# DISCOVER
# YOUR OTHER SELF

# Discover Your Other Self

## The Key to Unlocking Your Potential

REGGIE WATERMAN

# ACKNOWLEDGEMENT

THIS BOOK WOULD NOT HAVE been possible without God. Whether or not you believe there is a God is up to the sole discretion of the individual, but it is my duty to show gratitude in "The Source" that I am connected with.

The whispers that I received from God that one morning in March of 2020 has led to this publication. Through his direction I have been able to meet and converse with individuals that impacted my life in some shape or form.

Thank you, God, for the blessings, the opportunities and the hardships. All these events have led me to this very moment and the book will be used as a seed to deliver a message to the masses that will help others discover their purpose and renew faith in your existence.

May this book transform the lives of millions and bless the hands of everyone that touches it.

Hearts and eyes of many will be open to witness their own greatness and desires.

This is my declaration and testimony that God is in the process of manifesting my dreams. These dreams are now turning into reality.

I declare this manifestation in the name of Jesus Christ. Amen.

# WORDS FROM THE DISCOVER YOUR OTHER SELF COMMUNITY

*"I love Reggie's real-talk on DYOS because he discusses the deeper issues people often feel, but don't want to discuss on a live show. At its core, his show is about inspiring people to think in different ways and to keep moving forward."*

— **Wendy Glavin**

*"Discover Your Other Self (DYOS) brings very real and in-depth topics and ideas to the forefront all while having fun and making you feel right at home."*

— **Pedro Maciel**

*"Reggie is one of the best inspirational personalities anyone could follow! His shows are raw and authentic, with the opportunity to impact your life for the better."*

— **Melody Belliveau**

*"I was iffy at first about checking out DYOS, but I can certainly say it is one of the big reasons I broke out of my shell and became more driven to help support my peers health and wellbeing in my own creative way!"*

— *Eric Labancz*

*"DYOS has been an eye opener. Great guests and topics that he covers on his show relate to my everyday life. Its taught me to be myself and given me tips on how to interact with people within my industry. Watching his show has given me more confidence in not limiting myself and pushed me to go after different opportunities that I normally wouldn't even consider."*

**– Roy Seelall**

*"It has a calming effect on me, a type of self-care that I now look forward to every Thursday evening. DYOS truly is a great experience. I recommend this show as a valuable option to meet, greet, learn, have fun, and grow."*

**– Abby Jules**

*"Many times, after the event I find myself immediately watching the replay and reading the comments. So, discover your other self now by joining Reggie Waterman, his guests and the DYOS community at the next #DYOS event."*

**– Dale Wagner**

**© Copyright 2020 - All rights reserved.**

The content contained within this book may not be reproduced, duplicated or transmitted without direct written permission from the author or the publisher.

Under no circumstances will any blame or legal responsibility be held against the publisher, or author, for any damages, reparation, or monetary loss due to the information contained within this book, either directly or indirectly.

Print ISBN: 978-1-7778405-0-1
eBook ISBN: 978-1-7778405-1-8

Legal Notice:
This book is copyright protected. It is only for personal use. You cannot amend, distribute, sell, use, quote or paraphrase any part, or the content within this book, without the consent of the author or publisher.

Disclaimer Notice:
Please note the information contained within this document is for educational and entertainment purposes only. All effort has been executed to present accurate, up to date, reliable, complete information. No warranties of any kind are declared or implied. Readers acknowledge that the author is not engaged in the rendering of legal, financial, medical or professional advice. The content within this book has been derived from various sources. Please consult a licensed professional before attempting any techniques outlined in this book.

By reading this document, the reader agrees that under no circumstances is the author responsible for any losses, direct or indirect, that are incurred as a result of the use of the information contained within this document, including, but not limited to, errors, omissions, or inaccuracies.

Stories derived from individuals mentioned in this book are summaries of conversations and/or interviews that have been conducted on the "Discover Your Other Self" Season 1 and 2 that is readily available on LinkedIn and YouTube.

# TABLE OF CONTENTS

Introduction ............................................................. 1

Meet the Author ..................................................... 3

Chapter 1: I Hit Rock Bottom! ................................ 5

    **Can We Live Without Social Groups?** ............ 10

    **Overcoming Challenges of
the Social Recession** ............................................ 11

        The Birth of Discover
Your Other Self (DYOS) .................................. 11

        Spiritual Support ............................................. 14

        Personal Care .................................................. 15

    **Timothy Muttoo's Story** ................................... 16

    **Impossible is Nothing!** ..................................... 18

Chapter 2: The Pains ............................................. 20

    **The Pains Associated with COVID-19** ......... 22

        Post-Traumatic Stress Disorder ...................... 22

        The Pains on the Economy ............................. 24

    **Glenn Lundy's Story** ....................................... 25

        Life Tips .......................................................... 27

    **Brian Schulman's Story** .................................. 28

    **What Are Your Pains?** .................................... 30

**Chapter 3:** Hidden Pains in Relationships ... 32

**The Moment of Release** ... 36

**COVID-19 and Intimacy** ... 36
   How to Cope ... 38

**Veronica Owusu's Story** ... 39
   Life Tips ... 40
   Give Yourself Permission to be Happy ... 41
   Activity ... 41

**Lila Smith's Story** ... 42
   Life Tips ... 45

**Chapter 4:** I am a Survivor ... 46

**COVID-19 and Compromised Individuals** ... 49
   Social Injustice and Inequalities ... 49

**Kristin Sherry's Story** ... 50
   Activity ... 53

**Jahmaal Marshall's Story** ... 54

**Cabbie Richards' Story** ... 55

**Don't Let Discrimination Define You** ... 56

**Chapter 5:** Don't Stop Dreaming ... 58

**What is Your Vision?** ... 58
   Vision Statement ... 60

**How To Achieve Your Vision** ... 62
   Focus More on the "Why" than the "What" ... 63
   Keep Your Ambitions to Yourself ... 64
   Put Everything into Place ... 65

**The TIME Matrix** ... 66

| | |
|---|---|
| **Daniel Joseph's Story** | 68 |
| Life Tips | 70 |
| Activity | 70 |
| **Melanie Rousseau's Story** | 71 |
| **Chapter 6:** The Turn-Around | 74 |
| **Resilience is Key** | 76 |
| **Jerome Samuels' Story** | 78 |
| The Art of Building Resilience | 80 |
| **Passing Over Opportunities Repeatedly (POOR)** | 81 |
| Identifying Opportunities | 82 |
| **Opportunities Created Through Adversities** | 83 |
| Turning Adversities into Opportunities | 84 |
| Seizing Opportunities | 85 |
| **Sara Nathanson's Story** | 87 |
| **Chapter 7:** You Too Can Survive | 89 |
| **The Law of Attraction** | 91 |
| The Power of Your Mouth | 92 |
| Build Positive Connections | 93 |
| Celebrate Accomplishments | 93 |
| Read Inspiring Content | 94 |
| **Johnny Earle's Story** | 94 |
| Life Tips | 95 |
| **Chapter 8:** Building New Muscles | 97 |
| **COVID-19 and the Quest for Truth** | 98 |
| **X-FACTOR WORKSHOPS** | 100 |
| **My Gratitude** | 102 |

**Conclusion** 104

**References** 107

# INTRODUCTION

As I grew up, I heard the saying, "Life is never easy. It is a battlefield for the brave." This quote didn't fully make sense until 2019, when I hit my own version of rock bottom. I realized that life is packed with circumstances that unleash the bravery that is in each and every person.

In simple terms, bravery is a display of courageous behavior. The only reason why you might think that you are not brave is because you have not allowed that courageous behavior to be exposed. There are certain triggers that can bring forth that brave version of yourself. Sometimes, it takes difficult circumstances and situations to draw out glimpses of bravery.

This brings us to the fact that there are two versions of every being, the less resilient one that usually operates until the difficult moments arise and the resilient one that can cruise through whatever life may bring. The former is usually what we know about ourselves all the time, and the latter we usually have to discover.

"Discover Your Other Self" (DYOS) is a reflection of that moment when circumstances force you to uncover your resilient self. That hour when friends and family cannot do much for you other than to tell you, "Things will get better." That moment when the universe seems to be working against you. That second when you can't understand why all of your endeavors seem to fuel your situation towards worse conditions. I know you can relate to that moment, when you see all doors shut right in front of you and you get stuck in a dark and empty room with nothing and no one else to call on except for God.

2019 was my personal COVID-19. Many of the factors that were present or more prevalent during the first phase of the pandemic reflected that part of my life. No one could have guessed the devastation that COVID-19 would cause as it destroyed millions of lives in its wake. The sudden spread of this innocuous disease caught most people off-guard. As a result, the coronavirus left tens of millions of people ill, without work or the ability to afford the proper healthcare they so desperately needed. Besides this, hospitals had been flooded with patients seeking medical support. The barrage of patients pushed health care services beyond their limit, resulting in many shortfalls in personal protective equipment (PPE), beds in health care facilities, and health care staff on the ground.

In this book, I will take you on a journey through real life events that served as obstacles at the time, but later became the catalyst that helped me discover my other self. You will also be presented with other stories of people who have willingly told their own stories through my live show on LinkedIn called Discover Your Other Self (DYOS). The common denominator for all these stories is the role that hardships and challenges play in triggering the other self into action as well as encouragements that will leave you wondering, "What can't I do?" rather than, "What can I do?" It is my desire that you derive courage from these stories and embark on a journey to discover your purpose, not only for your well-being, but for the impact you will have on others and the world.

# MEET THE AUTHOR

Reggie Waterman has always been the odd man out. Even in his early days in elementary school, Reggie was among a handful of black students. In fact, he was one of three black students in his grade. This concept of being the odd man out followed him throughout his career as he strived to climb the corporate ladder.

Reggie is a single father of two children and has been forced to juggle the joys of fatherhood with the ongoing pressure from his ex-girlfriend who relentlessly strives to put a wedge between the kids and their father. After many costly court battles, Reggie was no further forward in his endeavors to see his children more regularly. The distraught father cannot make cell phone contact with his eighteen-year-old son because the young man's mother changed his cellphone number multiple times in a bid to prevent any father-to-son contact.

After serving 12 years in the telecommunications industry, Reggie hit rock bottom after he secured a job with a competing company and his efforts were aborted due to interference from the company that he had previously worked with. This action left Reggie unemployed, yet he still had to meet his financial obligation for child support while still managing his monthly bills and responsibilities at the same time.

The best part of these emotionally, psychologically,

and physically draining challenges became the catalyst to Reggie's journey of self discovery. As a result, Reggie has not only turned his life around, but he is on what he believes to be a divine mission to help others unlock their talents for success and achieve their true desires. Reggie also created a series of workshops that aim to develop the future leaders of tomorrow by giving them the tools they need to succeed post-graduation.

He lives by the mantra of "Constantly keeping you in wonder". It's a mantra that promotes the idea of creating greatness in everything you do while maintaining a sense of curiosity that leads to innovation.

# CHAPTER 1:
## I HIT ROCK BOTTOM!

It all happened suddenly. The year began in a normal way, just like any other year. I had been working in the telecommunications industry for a long time, 12 years to be exact.

I was working for a company where, despite all my efforts and diligence, success was only a dream. Many factors were supportive of this notion, which is the ultimate reason why I finally decided to quit.

1. My boss was horrible. He never wanted to promote me. He stole my ideas, did not give me credit for my efforts, and he never supported me when I identified foul play within my own team. He was also jealous of a friendship that I had with another woman that was on my team.

2. The company did not promote black people. There was no black representation in the higher levels of the organization.

3. They wanted to keep me in a box by preventing me from being creative and innovative.

Before I left the organization, I had secured a job with one of the company's competitors. I decided to resign right after returning from a work trip. When I told my boss that I was leaving for the competition, he was really upset, even going as far as to say that I would regret making this move. He also contacted his boss who eventually reached out to me and asked me why I was quitting. To make matters worse, he even asked me how much money the competitor was going to pay me. Upon telling him how much it was, he was shocked and exclaimed, "That's how much I pay my Directors!" I was only a Senior Manager at the time, so you can imagine how underpaid I was considering that another company was willing to compensate me fairly.

When I started orientation week at my new job, I got pulled of training by a Human Resources Manager. She asked me if I had downloaded information when I left my previous company, because my former boss had corporate security come after me. I had downloaded some of my old projects and information, and because of this, they got both of their legal teams involved.

I wasn't planning to use the information to be destructive. Besides, any average worker that usually leaves a company takes their previous work as an archive, just like I did. However, my previous employer deliberately did what they did so that I could lose my job at my new company. They also accused me of attending strategic meetings at the work trip that I had attended, which was not true. The case was investigated for almost a week. As a result of the investigation, my new employer decided to terminate my employment status, a decision which left me unemployed for the first time in my life. My previous employer and boss won that battle and they were proud.

## DISCOVER YOUR OTHER SELF

As painful as it was to receive the devastating news that I was no longer able to work for the new employer, I want to recount the ironic moments that occurred that very day.

I remember like it was yesterday. I woke up and prepared to go to my new place of work. I took a train from the suburbs where I live to the new workplace that was located in downtown Toronto. Upon arriving downtown, I got off the train and started to move towards the subway along with a sea of people who were walking in the same direction as me. The sea of people resembled the rat race which, to me, represented an unpleasant way of life where people would rush off to their daily jobs that don't usually serve them any purpose outside of paying their bills. I can't generalize, but I believe that most people live this way. Usually, there is no personal fulfillment and satisfaction in the rat race. Instead, it's all about who can get to work the fastest and climb the corporate ladder as a means to live out someone else's dream.

> **THERE IS NO PERSONAL FULFILLMENT AND SATISFACTION IN THE RAT RACE.**

As I continued to walk, I heard a voice that said, "Take a picture of this moment," so I obliged. I took out my phone and captured the moment. As I looked at the picture that I had taken, I heard another voice and this time it said, "Do you want to do this for the rest of your life?" My interpretation of the question was whether I wanted to remain part of the overall rat race. Was that the life that I wanted? I didn't answer the question at that moment and I continued to walk toward the subway.

Immediately after I received news that my new employer

decided to let me go, I walked across the street to my friend Dameon Wilson's workplace to ask if we could grab a coffee. I felt that I needed someone to talk to, because the world had become dark, and Dameon was the best person I could think of because he had been down this road before. When I met Dameon, I told him the news that the opportunity that I was so much looking forward to was no longer going to work out. Without any hesitation, he smiled. This triggered a bunch of thoughts in my mind. I couldn't really tell whether I was annoyed or surprised at his reaction, but I thought, "Why is he just smiling? Doesn't he understand that I'm hurting right now?" My world had just crumbled before my eyes and there he was, smiling. After his smile came a slight chuckle, before he proceeded to say, "This is the best thing that could have ever happened to you." Again, this reaction compounded my existing emotions. "I have bills to pay and I'm paying crazy amounts of child support. How am I going to make this work? What do you mean by 'this is going to be the best thing that could have ever happened to me?' This is horrible!

What are the first things that would come into your mind if you had just been informed that your employment status is null and void? You would think, "How am I going to pay my bills? How am I going to fend for my family?" These were the first questions that I asked myself, too. Already, the future had become more uncertain than it naturally is. What was I going to do?

> **"THIS IS THE BEST THING THAT COULD HAVE EVER HAPPENED TO YOU."**

## DISCOVER YOUR OTHER SELF

Mind you, I had never been unemployed before. I had been a high performer who always got promoted for putting in hard work and exceeding expectations. So here I was, beginning my first experience as an unemployed citizen.

Dameon further explained by telling me about a time where his unemployment status impacted him and how it turned out to be the best thing for him. Another key point that he made was, "God will show you what he can really do for you," and that I was going to develop skills that I never thought I had. Dameon told me his stories about how he journeyed through unemployment in a bid to give me insights into things that were to come. At the time, it was hard to process and come to terms with it because I was going through a grieving process. As I travelled back home after my discussion with Dameon, I realized why the picture that I had taken earlier on was so ironic.

> "GOD WILL SHOW YOU WHAT HE CAN REALLY DO FOR YOU"

Remember the picture that I took that resembled the rat race? When I thought about it some more, that was one of the things I dreaded the most. Everyone looked like they were zombies dragging their feet, going to jobs that they don't even enjoy. Although I was in excruciating pain from the loss of my job, I knew deep inside me that I didn't want to be lining up for a train, fighting to get a seat, or bumping into people as they cut me off while I walked to work.

One other thing that is worth noting is that although what Dameon said was not making much sense to me at the time, just having someone to talk to for support was a form of therapy in itself. I realized how true it is that human beings are social beings. We thrive better when we interact with others. This same aspect of the value of social interaction has also been evident during the COVID-19 pandemic.

## CAN WE LIVE WITHOUT SOCIAL GROUPS?

Before the COVID-19 pandemic, there were ways in which we used to show each other how much we cared. These methods had positive impacts that are difficult to replace even with virtual social interactions. Imagine how powerful a hug from a friend would be in the event that you would have lost a loved one. That rubbing, the pat on the shoulder, the gaze in each other's eyes in close proximity, the offers for tissues to dry tears that represented shared pain, was what kept us stronger in the face of adversities. The elbow-to-elbow greeting can never replace the dignity that was embedded in the common handshake. The handshake was symbolic of unity and respect for each other. Even a simple high-five is gradually being listed among known taboos as the fear of contracting the coronavirus dominates.

Social groups are safe havens for all living beings, humans included, and this has been evident during the COVID-19 pandemic. For millennia, humans have been conditioned to the importance of safety, nurturing, and supportive aspects of living in groups. Without these social structures, the rise in stress levels cannot be overstated. Stress causes the body to release a hormone called Cortisol. Cortisol is a good hormone that helps with the regulation of metabolism, reduction of inflammation, and increased memory (Hormone Health Network, 2018). However, too much Cortisol is also associated with conditions such as high blood pressure, muscle weakness, mood swings, and headaches (Santos-Longhurst, 2018). These conditions can amount to premature death.

No one can predict with any accuracy how the isolation due to COVID-19 impacts all individuals. One thing is for sure, the longer the period of separation and isolation, the more likely the quality of life among those at higher risk of depression and anxiety is going to decrease.

## OVERCOMING CHALLENGES OF THE SOCIAL RECESSION

The COVID-19 pandemic forced numerous businesses to adopt the concept of working remotely from home while staying in touch via video or virtual conferencing. Families have also resorted to using this method of communication to keep in touch with their loved ones. This technologically innovative way to remain in contact beats emails or even voice notes as it gives a better feel of each other's presence. Sadly, those who are usually affected more during challenging times such as the pandemic are people who are technologically compromised.

## THE BIRTH OF DISCOVER YOUR OTHER SELF (DYOS)

One morning in March 2020, while almost the entire globe was under lockdown, I woke up and said my prayers. After praying, I remember walking down the stairs, and all of a sudden, I had to stop. I had felt this presence and heard a voice talking to me, but I was all alone in the house. I believe that it was God who was talking to me. The voice was telling me, "Connect with the people."

I had no idea what this really meant, but I eventually put two and two together and decided to create a virtual community. I didn't know how I was going to complete this task, because I never did this before. The scenario was similar to how Noah received instructions to build the ark. Noah didn't realize that he was equipped with the tools until he started to build the ark.

As I kept thinking about the experience that I had with the voice, ideas started formulating in my mind. As a result, I created an event on Eventbrite and started reaching out to people, inviting them to a Zoom meeting to simply connect and network. I didn't have a clue what we were going to discuss if they showed up, but I said to myself, "If only one person shows up, that's all that matters." I would have had that conversation with that one person in hopes to create impact. Surprisingly, 28 people showed up at the first event. Two months later, I was hosting over 70 people on Zoom. It was magical!

Who is this other self? I grew to realize that there are two versions of the same person. There is a person in you that is uncomfortable with change. This is the person who operates when all is well, and it is also the same person who crumbles in the face of adversities. When you are in a tough situation that requires you to be strong, enduring, and

> **THIS OTHER SELF DOESN'T IMMEDIATELY COME TO THE SURFACE. IT WAITS FOR YOUR PERMISSION.**

## DISCOVER YOUR OTHER SELF

resilient, you will need to use the other self. Unfortunately, this other self doesn't immediately come to the surface. It waits for your permission. In other words, one decides whether they want to tap into another dimension of their being. When you decide to give into adversity, you fall into default mode, but the moment you decide to fight back and get back on your feet, you trigger your other self.

Therefore, the main purpose of DYOS was to establish a virtual community, help people overcome struggles, and to let people know they are not alone. It was meant to be a platform for encouragement and to create a resilient spirit. Lastly, DYOS was meant to help people build their personal brand because when you discover your other self, you will automatically feel empowered to put yourself in a position to help and impact people's lives!

I have now moved away from hosting these events on Zoom and have transitioned to LinkedIn Live to broaden the audience. I even added a Disc Jockey to the show, DJ D Money. Even his appearance on the show came as a result of listening to another whisper from God, "Get DJ D Money on the show." This was a means to build excitement and a vibe that no one else has done on LinkedIn and it worked! For every stream we host we are able to generate 700 to 1,000 viewers. Compare that to the height of the Zoom events that reached just over 70 people. We knew we were on the path of creating greater impact.

In Spanish, Dios means God. Remember those voices saying to connect with people? That was God speaking to me as a reminder that this platform was established by his words.

*"What are you grateful for today?*

We start by asking ourselves what we are grateful for as our trademark on DYOS. We have realized that power lies in noticing the good things in our lives rather than just focusing on what is wrong. Focusing on the good things is a great way to tackle hardships by creating positivity.

## SPIRITUAL SUPPORT

During my own predicament, spiritual connection kept me going, and this can also apply to the COVID-19 era. Despite the restrictions on physical contact, we can still make a difference by praying for each other. Some churches resorted to doing virtual spiritual services as a means to maintain and build engagement with their congregation.

You do not necessarily need to be surrounded by a bunch of people in order to start praying for someone. Even when you are alone at home, you can pray for elders, neighbors, colleagues, friends, and children. This is a simple but powerful way of offering spiritual support. There are some people who are often forgotten when people pray for each other. These are children in orphanages, prisoners in jail, and residents in old people's homes. No one has to know, just pray for them. That is networking at a spiritual level.

We are all brought into this world to serve others. I ask God on a daily basis to use me as a vehicle to deliver a message, to leverage my experiences so that I can be an inspiration for others. I have discovered that when you go down this path, the universe starts to open up to you. People, things, opportunities will be presented in a way where you often question how or why. It's because God is using you as an instrument to bring joy to others. This is what it truly means to pay it forward.

## **PERSONAL CARE**

Being in isolation and working from home can blur the lines between our normal daily activities and those we should employ for good self-care. One of the basic strategies for preventing the spread of the virus is undoubtedly to take good care of ourselves. We can do this by eating a balanced diet, embarking on a regular exercise routine, getting enough sleep, and staying positive.

Scrolling down the news all day long to see the death rates is not a healthy way of taking care of yourself. Spending most of your time watching television is not healthy either, and it is not healthy for your children. How about some indoor games like chess? You could just as easily play some hide and seek with your children to reduce their screen time which is bad for their eyes as it causes nearsightedness (Cimberle. 2020). Too much screen time can also expose children to harmful information over the internet.

The concept of personal care reminds me of the time when I broke my hand while playing basketball. This was at the same time that I was unemployed, so not only was I out of work, but I also had a broken hand. I thought that breaking my hand meant that I couldn't participate in CrossFit, which I had become passionate about, but I was wrong.

A friend of mine, by the name of Nicholas Waddell, told me about an audiobook called *Can't Hurt Me* by David Goggins. In *Can't Hurt Me*, ex-Navy Seal David Goggins shares his life story and experience of becoming a Navy Seal. The main premise of the book was to teach the reader about building a callous mind, meaning that whatever life challenge is thrown at you, you must build a strong mindset that will help you overcome any challenge. Since I had broken my hand, I still needed to be active because I didn't want to put on more weight, so I took up running. As I ran, I drew my inspiration from David Goggins' audiobook. I hated running, but as I ran, I would hear David Goggins in my ear, and he would often reference what it meant to be a "bitch" (his words, not mine!).

After I had been running for a while, something weird started to happen. I would often notice someone walking a three-legged dog. I took it as a symbol of overcoming life's limitations that we tend to put on ourselves. The masses refer to this as limiting beliefs. I believed that with a broken hand, I couldn't participate in the CrossFit Games, but that was my limiting belief. The reality was that I *could* participate in the CrossFit Games. See the difference?

I had decided to take a break from CrossFit, but after seeing this dog it made me realize that if that dog with three legs could walk on the path every day, then I could participate in the CrossFit Games with one arm, and so I did. Though I didn't place that high in the competition, I won an award and was recognized by my local gym for my grit and willingness to continue to keep going against all odds. Therefore, personal care is not only important for your body but also for your mind.

## TIMOTHY MUTTOO'S STORY

There are some people who cannot afford the technology involved in communication, let alone clean drinking water. However, they can be helped by those who have the motivation to impact the lives of others. This could be during, before, or after the pandemic. I hereby introduce to you a man who defied all odds and pursued his passion for being with those people who are often forgotten. Unlike me, who was forced into unemployment by circumstance, this man resigned from his well-paying job as a chemical engineer even before he knew what his next step toward his passion was. He simply left even when bills still needed to be paid and food had to be put on the table.

Timothy Muttoo says, "Sometimes our aspirations are so unique that no one is going to listen to you." That was the case with him when he decided to quit his job despite the fact that it would lead him to an unknown destination. But there was a driving force within Timothy. He felt that he wanted to act on his true calling even after all titles and all the other things had been removed. Timothy wanted to be known for how he treated men, women, and children. Therefore, with his gift of connecting with people, Timothy kept his sights on his passions for charity. Eventually, he made connections that led to the realization of his dream. It wasn't easy, but he soldiered on. Before he embarked on realizing his dream, he met naysayers along the way. However, despite what the naysayers said, Timothy didn't let them stop him.

> "SOMETIMES OUR ASPIRATIONS ARE SO UNIQUE THAT NO ONE IS GOING TO LISTEN TO YOU."

Timothy is now the co-founder of H2O4All, and his company has saved many women from the sex trade by providing clean water in exchange for their lives. Through H2O4All, Timothy has also met with presidents of different countries. How many of us can say that they had the privilege of meeting one president of a country let alone multiple?

Here are some things that I personally learned from Timothy's story as I interviewed him:

- Connect with your inner being. That is when you will realize your beliefs and passions.
- There are people out there who don't care about electronics, cellphones, or anything else. They are illiterate and impoverished. All they want is to know that someone cares.
- The most content people are those without anything, because they have learned to connect with who they are. When you have things, you tend to want more and lose connection with who you really are in the process.
- You should have a toolbox for life. This is where you put all the attributes and things that you need to turn your passions into reality. Some of these things might not work immediately, but you will need them someday.

## IMPOSSIBLE IS NOTHING!

"Impossible is nothing" is not an easy mindset to adopt, yet it is very crucial. I learned this the hard way, and I believe that this is what happens to many people. The first thing that you need to do in order to adopt this powerful mindset is deal with your subconscious mind. You first must "unknow" your old self so that you can get to know your

## DISCOVER YOUR OTHER SELF

true authentic self. In other words, remove those ideas that you thought defined you and make the effort to redefine yourself. Shed all of your limiting beliefs and replace them with "unlimiting" ones.

Second, promote yourself to be the director of your own movie, which is a metaphor for life. Remove your focus from what people think and direct your focus on how you want your movie to end. It's all about you. *You* are the director of your own life. You are in total control. Finally, take action and get yourself out of the trap of thinking that you aren't capable of doing or achieving anything that you want to.

> **SHED ALL OF YOUR LIMITING BELIEFS AND REPLACE THEM WITH "UNLIMITING" ONES.**

## CHAPTER 2:
### THE PAINS

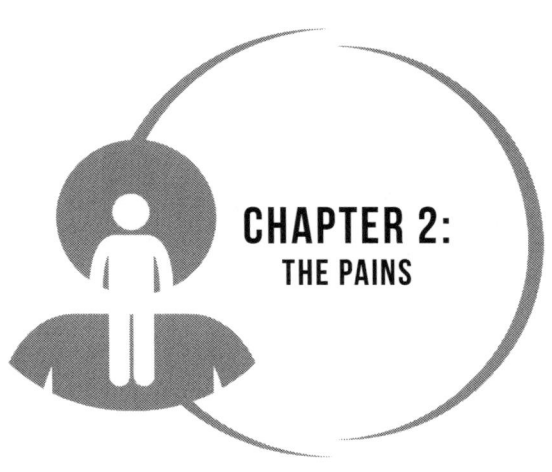

Just that one experience of losing a job put me through so much pain that I had never imagined I could experience. I had to update my resume over and over again, but it still seemed like my efforts were not good enough. Updating my resume, searching for job opportunities, then applying for those opportunities, to then receiving rejection letters pre- and post-interview became part of my daily routine. It was a painful cycle of emotions.

Everyone that I knew was busy with their own jobs and their own life. Mind you, it was not yet the COVID-19 era and there were no lockdowns. My friends would all go to work and I had to stay home to deal with my problems. I felt so isolated, hopeless, and worthless. Most of the people who wanted to know about my predicament were not really concerned about what I was going through. Rather, they wanted to know how I ended up being unemployed. I could feel people's negative perceptions piercing me. I felt too ashamed to get into the details.

I began to feel like a failure. It felt as though I had never done anything good in my whole life, which was not true. Everything had been wiped out by one bad mistake.

## DISCOVER YOUR OTHER SELF

I used to be very confident as I excelled in everything that I did. I have always been the odd man out, but in positive ways. This time around, self-doubt was creeping in, and I couldn't look at myself through a better lens other than the lens of failure. I felt lost and hopeless.

As I mentioned before, to add insult to injury, I broke my hand while playing basketball. This was extra pain that I had to bear, together with the uncertainty of whether I was going to be able to work out, let alone participate in the annual CrossFit games with one arm. Moreover, imagine now having to go to in-person interviews with a broken hand, pushing your bulky cast through the sleeve of your blazer, and having to tell the story of how you broke your hand over and over again to every hiring manager. It looked like I was losing virtually everything that mattered to me. I often found myself asking God, "Why is this happening to me?"

One day, I randomly met this recruiter on LinkedIn. Let me tell you this was truly a humbling experience. She countlessly criticized my resume, made me second guess my career choices and value that I had to offer the marketplace. It's like she was kicking me when I was already down and out. Here I was thinking, I have 10 plus years' experience in my respective field, I'm smart and I have a great smile, what's not there to like?

The recruiter really cut me down to size, but in a good way. What I thought were direct insults was really the constructive criticism I needed to reinvent myself.

> **I OFTEN FOUND MYSELF ASKING GOD, "WHY IS THIS HAPPENING TO ME?"**

After that encounter with the recruiter, I now realize that this recruiter transformed my resume into a powerful tool that could take me to higher places. It was through all of these experiences that I began to understand that most of our profound breakthroughs are achieved after we have experienced some pain. This changed my perception of pain and challenges. It was then that I realized that there are two sides to every story that is told. Which one you choose to focus on is up to you. For example, in my case, on the other side of criticism and pain was a better and more powerful resume. However, the truth is that it takes grace and extreme effort for one to embrace the good side of the story when pain is involved.

## THE PAINS ASSOCIATED WITH COVID-19

It cannot be overemphasized that many lost their jobs during the COVID-19 era. Many families were left without financial stability as some companies retrenched their employees so that their salary payments would tally with the companies' revenues. Some companies completely shut down, thereby rendering millions of people jobless globally. The pains of uncertainty, job hunting, people's perceptions, and rejection that are associated with joblessness affected many, just as they did to me in 2019.

## POST-TRAUMATIC STRESS DISORDER

The incredible overlap of serious threats such as loss of income, the death of loved ones from COVID-19, loss of

## DISCOVER YOUR OTHER SELF

homes, and an enormous down-swing in personal health appeared to have created a frightening scenario of stress-related illnesses that has never been seen before. So many people lost their businesses completely while some were hanging on by a thread but managed to weather the storm. These are difficult moments because it usually takes a long time to successfully establish a business entity and imagine all the efforts going down the drain.

Looking back at the financial slump in 2008, the number of suicides increased alarmingly. An increase in the suicide rate is expected during the pandemic and even in the post-pandemic period. There is no doubt that the stress levels that are caused by the pandemic can cause highly negative effects on health or even cost others their lives. However, I still maintain that in everything, your choice matters. Choose to trigger your other being and go against the odds. Would you rather give up, die, and leave your children to remember you as the "man that was too scared to live?" Or would you rather choose to live and let them embrace the hero in you? Later in this chapter, I will share with you a story of a man who nearly took his own life but later lived to tell a great story.

> **WOULD YOU RATHER GIVE UP, DIE, AND LEAVE YOUR CHILDREN TO REMEMBER YOU AS THE "MAN THAT WAS TOO SCARED TO LIVE?" OR WOULD YOU RATHER CHOOSE TO LIVE AND LET THEM EMBRACE THE HERO IN YOU?**

We can fight against post-traumatic stress disorders and save potential suicide victims by encouraging them to communicate their anxiety and depression. A problem shared is half solved.

## THE PAINS ON THE ECONOMY

National and international trade was affected by lockdown restrictions that were posed on almost all countries. Both local and international trade reduced, and this led to lower economic growth. This was mostly because some business activities cannot be done online. For example, in sports, the athletes have to be physically present to play a game. This was unfortunately impossible in 2020 due to the need to adhere to regulations of social distancing. In fact, national and international events for wrestling, athletics, netball, rugby, football, skiing, cricket, and other sporting activities were postponed at regional, national, and international levels. Olympics and Paralympics were also postponed to 2021. The sports industry's global value was estimated to be $756 billion every year during the pre-COVID era (Bas et al., 2020). This value began to reduce during the first wave of COVID-19 in 2020.

During a time when most economic activity was suspended, it is unfortunate that all countries still had to use the funds that were available in their coffers to invest in fighting the vicious pandemic. This ranged from testing people, treating the infected ones, providing survival funds to the poor, old, and vulnerable, and other things that governments did to manage the effects of the disease as well as its spread. Test kits for the virus, protective clothing for health workers and other frontline workers also required money during a time when economic activity was at its lowest rate in years.

Factors such as people having to miss work, premature deaths due to the pandemic, and reduction in productivity have affected the overall economies of many countries. Some manufacturing companies slowed down activities of production due to disruptions in the supply chain that were caused by the COVID-19 crisis. Additionally, some factories were closed, thereby reducing the options that manufacturing companies had for their supplies.

Bars and restaurants, entertainment, and travel and transportation sectors were strictly closed during lockdowns, causing a lot of revenue to be lost in the process. These sectors are important in both national and international trade. Most countries depend highly on international trade which was disrupted as borders were closed to enforce traveling restrictions that were meant to contain the virus.

## GLENN LUNDY'S STORY

According to Glenn Lundy, homelessness was associated with invisibility. No one notices you and you cease to exist in the world. No one will give you a hug. People will avoid you because they don't want to feel guilty for not helping you. They are scared that you are going to ask them for money. They are not even sure if you are not going to rob them. That is homelessness.

Unfortunately for Glenn, homelessness led to hopelessness which led to deep depression, which led to suicidal thoughts, and finally to the attempt to take his own life. With much help from the tides that swept him to the shore after he had tried to drown himself in the ocean, there was Glenn lying on his back.

That was when he had revelations that changed his life. First, he saw how expansive the universe was and how small his problems were in comparison to the universe. Second, he had flashbacks of the past where something bad happened in his life. He then noticed that in all the past events, there were different people each time, but he was the constant feature in all the scenes. That was when Glenn realized that he was the catalyst for all his problems. The transforming thought that came into his mind at that time was, "If this is the case, then I can also be a catalyst to good things in my life." He shifted his mindset from seeing himself as a victim to being a victor.

This mindset gave Glenn a new look towards the pains of life. He joined the automotive industry where he identified a huge gap in how car dealerships operated. One day, he decided to write down all of the things that he hated about the automotive industry as a consumer and then as an employee. He then used these points to turn things around in the company that he worked for until they had an 800% rise in revenue within six years.

In 2018, Glenn saw a window where he could now work with owners and managers of different car dealerships across America to help them realize exponential growth. He decided to quit his well-paying job to tackle this new mission. Glenn attests to the fact that almost everyone thought he was crazy for taking that step because he was comfortable in his previous job and his

> **I AM NOT A VICTIM, BUT I AM A CATALYST.**

pregnant wife was about to give birth. However, it turned out that this was the best decision that Glenn had ever made as he now works with 36 car dealerships. Imagine the opportunity that he would have lost by clinging to his previous job. That was an act of bravery.

## LIFE TIPS

Glenn is the founder of *Rise and Grind*, where he inspires and teaches others to have a solid routine when they wake up. A solid routine should tap into the body, mind, and spirit. Here are the five steps that he recommends:

1. The snooze button is evil! It's like the antichrist. So don't touch it!
2. Avoid placing a priority on touching your phone as soon as you wake up. In his own words he says, "Whatever you have there can wait, I promise you."
3. Write down the things that you are grateful for and the goals that you are trying to reach.
4. Do whatever physical exercises that you prefer. An object in motion tends to stay in motion, and an object at rest tends to stay at rest. Keep the body moving, keep the heart pumping, and keep the blood flowing.
5. Pump some positive frequency into the world so that you impact other people's lives. Remember that humans are tripartite beings with the mind, body,

and spirit. The spirit part of you gives you the ability to create things and impact others.

Glenn also provided a very important lesson on time management. He said that he tries everything in his power to condense time. He emphasized how so many people would say, "I am going to spend more time with my family." Spending is not a positive word. Spending time could amount to wasting time. Rather, use the term "invest" and say, "I am going to invest time with my family." Time well-used is not spent, it is invested.

> "I AM GOING TO INVEST TIME WITH MY FAMILY. TIME WELL-USED IS NOT SPENT, IT IS INVESTED."

## BRIAN SCHULMAN'S STORY

Having been born weighing 1.5 pounds, Brian Schulman entered this world fighting for every breath in order to live. He had been born three months premature, and this was in the 1970s when there were fewer medical interventions available to aid premature births. During his preteens, Brian was diagnosed with a neurological disorder that caused him to have uncontrollable twitches and tics called Tourette's Syndrome. He felt the pains of being discriminated and ridiculed for his condition at school and in society.

Brian recalls events where he would cry to his mother, because he did not understand why everyone did not like him and why everyone would make fun of him. It's painful to realize that people with Tourette's Syndrome don't have any control over their tics and twitches.

Brian was given multiple forms of medication to manage his condition. However, Brian said that things got even worse because the medicine would make him feel less energetic and extremely sleepy. With the medication, he found himself sleeping, even during classes he attended at school. Imagine the pains that he went through for something that he couldn't control or change. In the 5th grade, Brian decided he would rather deal with the uncontrollable tics and twitches associated with Tourette's rather than continue to experience the side effects of his medicine. Therefore, he decided to stop taking the medicine and take up natural ways of dealing with his condition. That was when he adopted music, dancing, and comedy as alternatives.

Brian was lucky. He did not experience the discouragements others usually do when he opened up about his diagnosis. Many expected Brian's story to fit their own description of standing out, but it was really about blending in. He just wanted to be accepted for who he was and be a part of a supportive team. "I didn't want to stand out. I just wanted to fit in", Brian explains.

One day, Brian made the hard decision to go against all odds and post a video on LinkedIn to tell his story. Making the video was one thing, posting it was another. He had a really hard time making that video. It was five months before he was able to make the final push to record and post it. When he posted the video, Brian recalls how nervous he was about how others were going to react to his video.

> **"THAT WAS THE FIRST TIME THAT I FELT LIKE BEING WEIRD WAS NOT A BAD THING. IT WAS MY SUPER POWER!."**

He wondered what his fellow employees, colleagues, and people with whom he had done business with in the past were going to think. Amazingly, the responses that he got from the video post swept him over. There was so much positivity embedded in all the comments, and to think that he had waited to post this video for five whole months! Brian said, "That was the first time that I felt like being weird was not a bad thing. It was my super power!."

Brian's brave step opened many doors:

- His story was featured in Forbes.
- He was nominated as one of the top 50 most influential people on LinkedIn in 2020.
- He is known as the godfather of LinkedIn videos.
- He is one of the world's top video marketing experts.
- He was LinkedIn Video Creator of the year 2019.
- His shows are syndicated on a Smart TV network.
- He is traveling the world just to share his story and journey.

## WHAT ARE YOUR PAINS?

What are you going through at this very moment? What have you been through in the past? Whatever you are going

## DISCOVER YOUR OTHER SELF

through, is it more than the pains of being homeless and dejected? Is it something that you were born with and that you cannot do much about other than accepting and managing it? Everyone has their own version of hitting rock bottom, and your pains are worth mentioning too. Life is a power-packed movie with ups and downs, but don't forget that you are the director of your own movie. We call it "Life".

The decisions and choices that you make right now have a lot to do with how your life will end. Choose to be strong and live to tell your story so that someone can learn from it. If Glenn, Brian, and I can do it, you certainly can! The power is within you, embedded in your other self. One thing that I can assure you is that your pains are there to provide the right environment for you to unleash your other self. Remember what Dameon said to me when I lost my job, that "this was the best thing that could have ever happened to you." Your pains could be "the best thing that could have ever happened to you" too!

## CHAPTER 3: HIDDEN PAINS IN RELATIONSHIPS

Prior to February 2013, when my son was nine years old and my daughter was two years old, the mother of my children constantly pleaded for financial support for our kids' upkeep. At that time, I was still living with my parents, and the mother of my children was living with her mom and other family members - that amounted to nine people living under one roof (on her side).

Besides the fact that I had separated from my ex-girlfriend, the other reason that I was still living with my parents was that I was paying $900 per month in child support. Imagine paying $900 per month in child support on top of the other household bills using one income. Now imagine paying $2,000 per month. Could you, do it? I will explain where the $2,000 per month comes from later, but I want you to do the math in your head and see if you could do it with one income.

After the endless pleas for more assistance from the children's mother, I decided to find a way to rectify the issue. At the time our residences were 30 minutes apart, so

I always made it my responsibility to drive back and forth to see my kids depending on the schedules that we agreed upon with their mother.

Without telling her my plans, I decided to purchase a home that was seven minutes away from the children to reduce the stress that was involved in living 30 minutes apart on top of the 60-minute-long commutes to and from work every day. I then decided to surprise the mother of my kids with what I thought would be good news. Instead of her celebrating the house that I had purchased, she responded by saying, "If you can afford a house, that means you can give me more money." I was astonished! I told her that giving her more than $900 per month while paying for the new house at the same time was not feasible. She didn't care, all she wanted was more money, and she pressured me for a few weeks. She didn't care that the shorter distance between us meant that I could spend more time with the kids.

After the continuous attempts to pressure me into meeting her demands, I did not oblige. As a result, she served me court papers. Going through the court process was something foreign and hectic for me. I thought I was doing a good thing by moving closer to my kids since I would be able to help out and spend more time with them. Since she had brought me to court, I had to disclose my finances, assets, and everything else. It was during this process that I saw her ugly side. I wouldn't wish Family Court on my worst enemy. The process is grueling and is an utter insult to the meaning, "best interest" of the children. My interpretation of this process is to test your mental and physical health to the extreme. The mental breakdown was enhanced by the endless paperwork, lawyers, process servers, not to mention the people that work at these court offices. To make matters worse, I am a black male and there was this perception/stereotype that others had around black men having a "baby mama." It was like I could read the minds of every court official in that building, "Ah! Here's another black man in court for child support, what else is new?"

I still recall how, before obtaining a lawyer, I was representing myself during court appearances. I wrote an 80-page document (twice) outlining all of the events that demonstrated how the kids' mother tried to prevent me from seeing the kids. The end result of it all was that I had to pay more money for the children's support because everything is calculated based on your current salary. This meant that I was going to pay $2,000 per month for child support and daycare expenses. As a result, I wasn't able to move into my new house, and I had to rent it out to tenants. I was determined to do whatever it would take to live in that house, which I eventually did (years later). However, in the meantime, I remained at home with my parents until I could afford a basement apartment.

> "AH! HERE'S ANOTHER BLACK MAN IN COURT FOR CHILD SUPPORT, WHAT ELSE IS NEW?"

There were even times when my new relationship with another woman was impacted because the mother of my children was in a jealous rage. One time, I had my girlfriend watch over my daughter while I took my son to soccer practice. As soon as my ex found out that my girlfriend was watching my daughter, she fled from the soccer practice and went straight to my basement apartment. This caused havoc with my landlord who lived on the main floor as she attempted to call the police just to take my daughter from my girlfriend. However, when the police arrived on the scene, they realized that my daughter was not in any harm and labeled it as a false alarm. This was just one of many occurrences where she disrupted access to my children.

There were multiple occurrences where my access to the children was disrupted during Christmas. As we all know, Christmas is a time for family. Imagine having someone strip you of your rights to see your loved ones on Christmas day. How would you feel? Especially after you are paying $2,000 per month for children that you can't even spend time with.

My relationship, connection, and social situation were probably worse than the scenario that is presented by COVID-19. Although you cannot have physical interaction, you can still connect online through text messages, voice calls, and video calls with your loved ones. My case was worse. Neither physical connection nor online connection was feasible. It wasn't because I couldn't afford it, but because I was denied the opportunity to do so. During the time when I lost my job and had no means of survival jobwise, I still had to pay $2,000 per month for my children.

Mind you there are so many other situations that occurred throughout the years, but that would defeat the whole purpose of this book. This book is to help you maintain focus on achieving your goals through struggle and adversity.

REGGIE WATERMAN

## THE MOMENT OF RELEASE

Even after having gone through such painful experiences, I decided to release myself from the pains of life using the art of seeking peace through forgiveness. I sent emails to people that I hurt in the past, asking them to forgive me. I sent one to the mother of my children, my ex-fiancée, an old friend, my sister, and two bosses from the previous employer that interfered with my employment. Only my sister, old friend, and mother of my children responded to my emails - the rest didn't. However, I still felt that I had done the right thing in the best way that I could. Sending the emails was a healing experience as I felt some level of relief and freedom from the past within me.

## COVID-19 AND INTIMACY

One of the fears that we have learned to live with from the time that COVID-19 was declared a global pandemic is what I would call "fear of the next person." You couldn't be sure if a person is a carrier of the coronavirus or not. You could even be a carrier yourself but won't even know it until you got tested. What if you got it from someone while going shopping for groceries or visiting a relative? Everyone became a possible "suspect."

The scenario that I have just given you already gives you a picture of what could have been happening in different homes. Although couples may be staying together, intimacy could be a problem amidst the pandemic. In one study which included 742 couples as respondents, 34% of the participants reported that they were facing reduced intimacy and increased interpersonal conflicts as compared to the pre-COVID era (Brenner, 2020). Instead, most respondents were resorting to options such as masturbation to replace the usually unavailable intimacy.

It was also noticed that those who reported increased conflicts with their partners were also highly affected by depression, stress, and loneliness. This is because of the compromised connection between partners.

In some cases, the reduced intimacy was not directly attributed to the fears that resulted from the existence of the pandemic. There is a tendency in human beings to have more conflict when they spend too much time together. The pandemic has brought more "stay at home" time, a state in which increased the time that families have with each other. This can be a good thing as most families never had the chance to experience so much togetherness due to the busy schedules that people have in the twenty-first century. However, chances for conflicts also increase with all of this time together. This then affects the intimacy of couples whose conflict management skills are based on refraining from intimacy. This usually happens in younger couples who

> **34% OF THE PARTICIPANTS REPORTED THAT THEY WERE FACING REDUCED INTIMACY AND INCREASED INTERPERSONAL CONFLICTS AS COMPARED TO THE PRE-COVID ERA**

would not have mastered more productive and assertive ways of resolving their conflicts.

Even where intimacy is reportedly present, there is less satisfaction, probably due to the increased tendency to cocoon themselves for fear of contracting or spreading the coronavirus. Actions such as kissing, hugging, and cuddling which people often used to show love for each other are currently less recommended because they provide a means of transmission of the coronavirus between individuals.

## HOW TO COPE

Intimacy is the main thing that brings and keeps couples together. It is likely you hadn't noticed that you have been gradually drifting further and further apart from your partner. Once you make this realization, you need to find ways of addressing your issues before it's too late. The first option that you could consider is to talk things over with your partner. Together, identify the causes of your conflicts and how they affect your intimacy. Brainstorm other ways that you can deal with your conflict rather than completely halting intimacy.

If you realize that you are not able to reach any agreements in your discussions or that the discussions could be worsening the situation, consider allowing someone else to help both of you. A good counselor or marriage advisor can act as the "middle person" to aid a calm discussion between you.

# DISCOVER YOUR OTHER SELF

## VERONICA OWUSU'S STORY

In the past, Veronica Owusu wanted peace. To attain this, she would live passively according to people's opinions of who she should be. In her own words, Veronica was not holding her own steering wheel. Veronica thought that she was destined to become a teacher, but later discovered that God had other plans. Together with her husband, they decided to pursue entrepreneurship as business partners in the import/export business. Unfortunately, this ultimately led to disappointment as the business crumbled. Selling their personal items at pawn shops to make ends meet became their way of life.

It didn't take much time before Veronica came to terms with the fact that not only was her business relationship not working, but her romantic relationship also followed suit. This was Veronica's own version of hitting rock bottom. She had to let go of the one she loved. Veronica says, "I had to forgive so that I could forgive myself. I had to give compassion so that I could give myself compassion."

Veronica recalls an incident when she was about to sell the last thing that they had when she heard a voice that told her to unleash her "caged warrior." When she lost virtually everything, that was the moment when she had to truthfully answer the question,

> "I HAD TO FORGIVE SO THAT I COULD FORGIVE MYSELF. I HAD TO GIVE COMPASSION SO THAT I COULD GIVE MYSELF COMPASSION."

> **THE TRUE DEFINITION OF ONESELF IS THE ONE THAT IS NOT DEPENDENT ON TITLES AND BELONGINGS.**

"Who am I?" Veronica emphasizes the fact that when you define yourself according to what you have, you are bound to lose confidence when you lose those things. Take note of these examples that she gave:

- "I am a wife." Who do you become when the marriage falls apart?
- "I am a manager." Who do you become when you lose your job?

Therefore, the true definition of oneself is the one that is not dependent on titles and belongings. Veronica is now a life coach at VPower where she helps people to create a ripple effect. In other words, she helps them so that they can help others. Veronica says, "I help people to discover the 'gold dust' within themselves and repackage it into something useful."

## LIFE TIPS

Here are some life tips from Veronica:

1. Deal with the imposter syndrome. The imposter syndrome is the inner feeling and experience that makes you see yourself as less competent as compared to how others see you. It is that "I am not good enough" feeling. Veronica deals with the imposter

syndrome by reminding herself what she has been able to accomplish.
2. When you decide to forge your way forward, do not leave everything that you were. It's fine, you have identified your real self and you want to live up to the person that you have discovered, but if you bury everything about your past, what if there is some of your "gold dust" in that? Unleash that because that is what will make you stand out and make a difference. Veronica's coaching is based on the experiences that she had. If she had buried everything, would she be doing her work the same way that she is doing it?
3. Give yourself permission to be happy. Quite often, when people go through hardships and tension, they tend to numb their emotions by not allowing themselves to experience these emotions. The result of this is that they literally imprison themselves.

## GIVE YOURSELF PERMISSION TO BE HAPPY

When you give yourself permission to experience the pain, it becomes easier to let go of the things that bring you back and cause the pain. When you don't let go, it is like allowing the thief to come into your home and steal your greatness.

## ACTIVITY

1. Ask yourself, "What do I think about relationships, business, or money?"

2. Whatever answer you get, also ask yourself, "Is this answer originally mine?" If not, where did it come from?
3. The last question should be, "Will this empower or cripple me?"

When you genuinely answer question two (2), your perceptions might be influenced by past experiences and other things. Things that you hold on from your past can either empower or cripple you. Therefore, the aim is to only allow past experiences that empowered you to stay and let go of past experiences that crippled you. Imagine a pipe that is clogged with a lot of things that are not supposed to be in there. Water cannot flow through, and the little that may flow through is more likely to be dirty. Unhealthy past experiences can hinder the smooth flow of life. The moment that you let go, life begins to flow.

> **UNHEALTHY PAST EXPERIENCES CAN HINDER THE SMOOTH FLOW OF LIFE. THE MOMENT THAT YOU LET GO, LIFE BEGINS TO FLOW.**

## LILA SMITH'S STORY

Lila Smith spent 20 years of her life as a scholar and actress. From her experience, she knew that whenever you stand on the stage, you must have an intention if you are to connect with the audience. You must have context as a character, and you have to make it real. Everything about her job evolved around intentions, but this was not the case at home.

Lila was in a relationship where her partner would do things that hurt her, and each time that she tried to open up and tell him that she had been hurt, the same answer always came up. He would say, "It wasn't my intention to make you feel that way." In other words, the answer was never apologetic, but rather it would shift the blame back to Lila. So, each time, she would feel diminished, belittled, unheard, or one of the worst, she would feel as though her emotions were the result of shortcomings on her part.

Most of the things that she would get from him were discouragements. "He would make me think like everything was possible for everyone else, except for me," said Lila. As time elapsed, Lila was increasingly becoming less confident, juggling with the efforts to become what she wanted to be while fighting the negativity that was coming from the person that she loved. She progressively became less aware of herself.

Lila's emotional degradation continued until one day, when her partner did something hurtful again and he was about to throw his usual bomb to say, "It was not my intention…" Lila did not let him finish his sentence. It was time for her to break even. She had to ask a new question, and this time the question was not, "Why did you do this?" It was, "Was it also not your intention to make me feel diminished, belittled, feel guilty…?" Lila was trying to bring out what her partner's usual answer was creating in her while killing her real self. She had to voice it before it was too late.

*"Ask new questions if you are tired
of the same answers."*

> **IT IS GREAT THAT YOU KNOW WHO YOU WANT TO BE, BUT WHO ARE YOU IN THE EYES OF THOSE WHO LOVE YOU, THOSE WHO YOU LOVE, AND THOSE WHO INVEST IN YOU?**

There is always an intention behind the words that we speak, especially to others, and it can only be either good or bad. If your words are not meant to make someone feel good, then automatically they are meant to make them feel bad. It is great that you know who you want to be, but who are you in the eyes of those who love you, those who you love, and those who invest in you? Whatever you say or do communicates your intentions to others, and this determines how they perceive you. Behave in a way that aligns with your values. Before you communicate, choose three action words that will define your values. These words literally describe the intentions behind your communication.

One other thing that we can learn from Lila is that she acknowledges what she is bad at, and that is key for any relationship. Lila said, "I am such a terrible apologizer," and she is still working on that. She describes her apologies as the "I am sorry, but..." type, and that kind of apology where one does not fully own their shortcomings is part of their mistake. Knowing yourself well enough to acknowledge where you need to make improvements is one of the best tools in making yourself better.

## DISCOVER YOUR OTHER SELF

# LIFE TIPS

Lila says,

1. Voice out. Most people stay silent, but the best thing that you could do for yourself and others is to speak up.
2. Whisper something to someone—something that will help them. When that person also whispers to someone else, you have three voices from one. With time, you will have ten, thirty, a hundred, or thousands of voices, but it all begins with one voice.

# CHAPTER 4:
## I AM A SURVIVOR

**W**HEN I FOUND MYSELF WITHOUT work and without any form of long-term survival, I realized I could fall no further than rock bottom. There were only two options available to me. The first option I could have chosen was to lie down and give up. The second option was to stand up, dust myself off, and start to climb towards finding success. After battling with my thoughts for some time, I chose the second option, although I had no idea of where I was going to start from. The first rung of the ladder to success seemed to be far from reach.

During the toughest times in my life, I wondered who I really was and what my real purpose in life was. I was not sure whether I was supposed to call this fate or a phase of life. The most difficult thing when you are in dark moments is to imagine seeing a light. I am referring to moments like when someone might tell you, "There is light at the end of the tunnel," but it feels that there simply isn't.

> **THE GREATER THE DIFFICULTIES YOU FACE, THE GREATER THE PRESSURE TO CHANGE.**

## DISCOVER YOUR OTHER SELF

All circumstances around you would be pointing towards complete loss of hope. Does what I am saying sound familiar to you?

Making the decision to live and get back up on my feet is one of the most difficult decisions that I made when I hit rock bottom. The reason why it is difficult is that everything around you will be citing negative scenarios. The only things that you may have that are positive are your words and your thoughts. Keeping them positive is a struggle on its own. Professor Ezekiel Guti wrote a book called *Humans Cannot Change Without Pressure*. The greater the difficulties you face, the greater the pressure to change.

> "'FOR I KNOW THE PLANS I HAVE FOR YOU,' DECLARES THE LORD, 'PLANS TO PROSPER YOU AND NOT TO HARM YOU, PLANS TO GIVE YOU HOPE AND A FUTIRE.'"
> JEREMIAH 29:11

It was not all without effort. I listened to Joel Osteen and Les Brown every morning, and their motivational speeches are part of what helped me through my darkest hours. Moreover, my mother would send me Bible verses from time to time. There is one particular passage that stuck out the most and this was Jeremiah 29 verse 11 which says, "'For I know the plans I have for you,' declares the Lord, 'plans to prosper you and not to harm you, plans to give you hope and a future.'" This Bible verse really kept me going.

Remember Nicholas? That same friend that introduced

me to David Goggins' audiobook? He also gave me a book called *The Alchemist* written by Paulo Coelho. Nicholas told me, "You have to read this! You are Santiago! You are on your journey to greatness." Santiago is the main character in the book. Nicholas also introduced me to the Wim Hof Method. The Wim Hof Method is a simple, but powerful, method that is based on the foundation of three pillars of breathing, cold therapy, and commitment (Wim Hof Method, 2019). It is a scientifically proven procedure that is about reconnecting us to ourselves, others, and to nature by stimulating deep physiological processes that help us to realize our full potential.

Different ideas began to formulate in my mind because now I had time to think. I couldn't contain these ideas in their abundance, so I had to write them down. Not only did I write them down, but I put them on post-it notes, which I would stick all over my bedroom wall. At times, it would look like I was trying to solve a crime and I was the detective! These ideas would eventually ladder up to specific goals that I wanted to attain along with associated actions that I needed to take. I posted them on my wall so that they were visible and I wouldn't miss them when I woke up. I realized the power of the subconscious mind as well as the daily affirmations, both of which were the concepts that I derived from Napoleon Hill's book, *Think and Grow Rich*. Ultimately, this became my favorite book of all time!

## COVID-19 AND COMPROMISED INDIVIDUALS

There are so many people who were in more compromised positions during the COVID-19 crisis. This could be by nature of being financially disadvantaged or by virtue of their citizenship, color, or by their abilities and disabilities.

In the face of COVID-19, the predicament of some people was double what they normally face because of discriminatory practices. For example, in government hospitals of some countries, whether you are a citizen or a foreigner determined how and when the health professionals would attend to you. The priorities of who to treat first were not based on the severity and urgency of conditions, but color, citizenship, and financial status.

It is unfortunate that most of the people who were victims of such situations are the same people who are financially disadvantaged and could not afford to pay the high bills that are required for them to access healthcare in private hospitals. Neither did they usually have access to medical aid facilities. Should we, then, allow our physical makeup to be the barrier to our success? Later on in this chapter, we will draw some strength and motivation from people who defied the odds of marginalization, discovered their other selves, and turned their lives around for the better.

## SOCIAL INJUSTICE AND INEQUALITIES

There has always been a clear demarcation between the wealthy and the financially disadvantaged people, and this worsened in the wake of the pandemic. For example, the wealthy have greater disposable incomes than the rest of the population. Most of the upper-earning echelon consists of highly educated professionals and managers who enjoy internet-ready facilities in their homes and places of work. Their children are more likely to have their own bedrooms well prepared for optimum study purposes and non-disruptive work-from-home situations. Many of these families, though also affected by the pandemic, are more likely to be able to continue life with fewer disruptions than the rest of society.

In the US, the wealthy make up for one percent of the population, and these individuals are better cushioned from the effects of the pandemic. In contrast, the rest of the people who make up ninety-nine percent of the population face the full wrath of the pandemic. Many of these families have been pushed to the limit of their resources and have nowhere to turn to for support. Due to the lack of internet facilities and other relevant resources, many children, even the most brilliant ones, may be unsuccessful in reaching their full academic potential. These are some of the negative effects of the digital divide, especially in pandemic times.

## KRISTIN SHERRY'S STORY

Have you ever felt like people's perceptions of who you are become barriers to your success? Kristin made reference to a variety of occasions in her life that labelled her as a misfit in society. First, she is half white and half mohawk. Her father is white while her mother is an indigenous person from Canada. Kristin was born in Buffalo, but lived in

Canada when she was a day old. Therefore, she was neither American because she didn't grow up there, nor was she Canadian because she was not born there.

Second, Kristin referred to herself as tomboy growing up as a kid, because she didn't like the style of clothing or activities that are normally associated with girls or seen as feminine. Third, fast forward into adulthood, Kristin worked in a male-dominated industry - Information Technology (IT), which also gave her the title of a misfit.

Kristin was known for being an enthusiastic person who was keen to try new things. She recalls a day when she was sitting in her office before her manager called her and said, "Kristin, you are too enthusiastic. You need to tone it down." Since then, she spent the next 15 years of her life trying to lower her enthusiasm and tried to be more "professional." She says, "I practically monitored myself into paralysis all because of one person's feedback." Sometimes, the feedback that we get from people is not constructive, just negative, and this puts you inside the box. It limits us.

There was a time in Kristin's career that she was dissatisfied with the trajectory and direction it was going in. She recalls the anxiety, the headaches and the stress she encountered from her job. It was through these occurrences that she was able to pin point and discover what she needed to be happy. Kristin's past experiences was the inspiration for developing the YouMap® assessment tool, which helped her to earn the 2020 Career Innovation Award. Kristin wanted people to experience this self-discovery for themselves that would help them to pursue the careers that were fulfilling to them.

Before she set her sights on formalizing YouMap®, Kristin needed to know what people hated about their jobs and what their ideal job would look like. So, she searched to see if she could find tools that were available in the market that could help her to do this. She found some competitive tests that would concentrate on one aspect or the other, like personality tests and strength value tests. There was nothing that brought everything together, so she set out to create one. That marked the birth of YouMap® which went viral up to a point that it spread into seven countries within two years.

Kristin's joy is derived from the fact that she has been able to contribute to the universe by helping people to discover their true selves and gain confidence. One testimony that Kristin got from one of her customers who had bought her book and did the YouMap® on his own read, "I am a 45-year-old IT guy. I am typing this message through tears. I did my YouMap® and I have seen why I have been so unhappy. I see myself for who I am for the first time in my life."

From this testimony, we are reminded of two things:

- Other people can see you and define you more clearly.

OR

- You can see yourself for the first time.

Kristin breaks down the notion of seeing yourself for the first time with an interesting analogy, "It is hard to see the label when you are inside the jar. You need to come out

## DISCOVER YOUR OTHER SELF

and see it from the outside, and this is what YouMap® helps you to do."

However, like any form of innovation, YouMap® was not without criticism. Researchers and other big companies were against a lot of aspects of the assessment. Kristin did not let that stop her. Her focus was on the testimonies that she received from the efficacy of the assessment. Two things helped her to get through all of this. First, she learned to separate her opinion from her identity. Second, she adopted the art of "eating the meat and spitting out the bones." In other words, focus on what you really want and let go of things that don't serve you.

> "IT IS HARD TO SEE THE LABEL WHEN YOU ARE INSIDE THE JAR."

## ACTIVITY

Here is an activity that Kristin suggests:

1. Look at your job and identify what is wrong.
2. What is it that you don't like? Are your values being violated?
3. What are the things that you can control or influence?
4. What is out of your control?

If you can control or influence the things that you don't like, then make the effort to influence. If it is out of your control, it is better for you to walk away from it.

REGGIE WATERMAN

## JAHMAAL MARSHALL'S STORY

Here is a black man that refuses to allow his skin color to put him at a disadvantage. Rather, he chooses to see it as an advantage. Jahmaal Marshall is a counselor who has touched the lives of many people. All of his efforts came in handy when he lost his father who was a best friend to him. Life became dark and there was less, if any, meaning attached to life at that time. Like they say, "The good you do, you do it for yourself, and the bad that you do, you do it for yourself." Despite the pain that he felt from losing his father, the lives that Jahmaal touched began to touch him back.

Here is what Jahmaal says about 'black privilege'.

- It all starts in the mind.
- "It's not about the breaths we take away, it's about the opportunities we take to take those breaths away." —Maya Angelou
- He says, "By virtue of my brown skin, I stand out. By being a content creator in a white space, that alone is good enough for me to take your breath away. Once the mindset is there, the body kind of follows."
- He says, "I have the privilege of 'not being entitled,' so I cannot be pretentious about anything. I am going to be myself. There is nothing to portray. Therefore, I bring my authentic self to any room that I come into."

We can learn from Jahmaal that you cultivate how you view yourself in your mind. You can choose to look at your differences as a disadvantage, or you can choose to look at your differences as an advantage. The trick here is the right mindset. What you do is not limited by your skin color or any other attributes.

## CABBIE RICHARDS' STORY

Toronto sports journalist icon Cabral Richards, who is also known as Cabbie, has had his fair share of stretching himself to break down racial barriers. In an industry dominated by white males, Cabbie prides himself in his unique approach of getting close and personal with the athletes that he interviews. Cabbie had the privilege to interview Michael Jordan, Aaron Rodgers, and the late great Kobe Bryant with whom Cabbie built special bonds. Cabbie's talents have enabled him to land several prestigious positions in the sporting world. Currently, he is an Executive Producer and On-Air Talent at Sportsnet.

In all of his endeavors, Cabbie believes in building relationships with people, especially if there is something that you want them to do for you. Cabbie explains, don't just pop a message and ask people to do you a favor without creating the foundation of a relationship. At least greet them. First, introduce yourself, and then talk about something else before you get to the point. Do you recall times when you probably sent a survey to all the people in your phonebook, some of whom you have never talked to at all? No greeting or anything and no explanation of what you are doing - just a bold statement asking them to complete the survey and send it back to you.

Time and money are involved when it comes to asking

people for favors. This is Cabbie's superpower. He creates, nurtures, and sustains good relationships with the people that matter in his career, and that has been his way of navigating through towards the top. He continues to use his superpower to this day.

## DON'T LET DISCRIMINATION DEFINE YOU

It seems that the coronavirus is not going to leave us in a rut, but even if it does, the challenges that it brought should trigger the best person within us. This, however, requires intrinsic motivation that defies all odds. Don't dwell on the discrimination and perceptions of other people, because if you do, those are the things that are going to define you and your future. Remind yourself that you are human. You have what it takes to step on the rungs of the ladder, one after the other, until you reach the top.

Let me share with you my personal story about discrimination at work. In a meeting with a former employer, we were brainstorming ways that we could build hype and drive traffic to our stores during Black Friday which is one of the busiest retail events of the year. One Vice President that was in the room said out loud, "I have an idea for Black Friday, we should put Reggie in the windows!" Everyone in the room started laughing. Being the only black person in the room, it was hard and uncomfortable for me to react in a way that would go against the majority. Obviously, this Vice President didn't think twice about how racially charged her statement was. This shows the ignorance and insensitive approach people have against matters of racial discrimination among minorities.

While you do not want to be discriminated against, also make it a point to refrain from discriminating against others. I believe that as long as we are able to change our perceptions, we are able to conquer all things, including all forms of discrimination. There are two ways through which we can do this. First, we could choose to view our differences in color, physical makeup, financial status, and languages as tools that make the world a better place. Second, focus on the fact that we are human beings, nothing more, nothing less, and that's all that matters.

> YOU HAVE WHAT IT TAKES TO STEP ON THE RUNGS OF THE LADDER, ONE AFTER THE OTHER, UNTIL YOU REACH THE TOP.

# CHAPTER 5:
## DON'T STOP DREAMING

"**Y**OU'VE GOT TO BE HUNGRY...WHATEVER anyone says about you is none of your business... Do the things that others won't do." That is Les Brown. Now, you understand why I have to mention him among my pillars of strength when I hit rock bottom. No matter how difficult things may be, keep dreaming and work towards the realization of your dream. The tools to make things happen are within you. It is your other self. That person within you that is daring - the person who defies all odds.

## WHAT IS YOUR VISION?

Do you know what your vision is yet? Maybe you prefer calling it an ambition or a dream. Whatever the case might be, knowing your ambition is important because it is, on its own, a motivation towards fulfilling your purpose in life. If you haven't discovered your vision yet or you want to redo the process of identifying your ambitions, I will take you through an exercise that will help you to do that. Here is how I define vision, as an acronym:

## DISCOVER YOUR OTHER SELF

**Visualize:** Identify what you want to achieve.

**Internalize:** Understand your goal and its uniqueness.

**Strategize:** Put in place the strategies that you will use to accomplish the goal.

**Initiate:** Set the arrangements to realize your goal by putting things in motion (taking action).

**Overcome:** Challenges are bound to come your way, but be determined to overcome them.

**Necessitate:** Find out what is necessary for you to get to your goal.

Here are some steps that you could consider in determining your vision:

**Begin with the little things:** It's only us who call them little things with a diminishing attitude, but those things really matter. Identify these little things that you desire to accomplish. Before you start, always remember that everyone has their own ambitions, and those are the ones that help us to accomplish our everyday tasks. It is easier for you to identify your ambitions if it is in your mindset to believe that you have them.

**Brainstorm:** Take some time to daydream and brainstorm so that you can unleash your vision. Ask yourself questions like, "What is my purpose in life?" "What do I value the most?" "What do I love to do?" and "What am I passionate about?" For each question, write down anything that you can think of, and I mean anything.

**Summarize, analyze, and revise:** When you have all of your ideas written down, the next thing is to attach realistic meanings to them. Begin by grouping points that are similar together. Once you have done that, write an umbrella statement that describes each group of ideas, and then expand on those statements to give them a specific focus. For example, one of my group statements could be, "I want to help people," but "helping people" is broad. Working as a nurse is helping people, and so is being a counselor. Is that what you mean? Do you see the reason why you should expand? I could say, "I want to help people to realize and identify their other self."

**Make it actionable:** This is when you should determine how you intend to accomplish what you have set yourself up to do. Put together clear and specific steps and make them exciting by connecting to them. Envision how you or others will benefit from what you want to do. Imagine your expected outcome and get excited to start the journey to accomplish your set ambition. Set time frames for achieving objectives that are connected to your main goal as well as the time frame to achieve your overall ambition.

## VISION STATEMENT

Make it a habit to write down a vision statement for your goal. This is a short paragraph where you state your desires. A good vision statement should include the following:

- Dates and timelines for accomplishing the goal

## DISCOVER YOUR OTHER SELF

- A clear description of the steps that you plan to take to accomplish the goal
- Make it visible by posting it on a wall where you can easily see it.
- Read it out loud - at least twice a day - in the morning when you wake up and before you go to bed.
- Envision yourself achieving your goal.

Here is a sample of a vision statement:

*I, Jane Doe, vow that on February 19, 2025, I will have a net worth of no less than $5 million. In return, I devote the next five years of my life to building tools and writing stories that will help others to reach their goals and live more fulfilling lives. My mission for the first year is to write 39 stories and learn to build my first tool. This is my life's purpose, and I commit my entire being to this realization.*

Do you see how specific this vision statement is? It has dates, timelines, and what is going to be done all laid out clearly. It is more probable that you will meet naysayers who will tell you, "You can't do this or that." It is normal to get negative feedback, even from yourself, but you need to understand this: most of the feedback is based on outer qualities. However, like an onion, we all have layers. If you unravel the layers, you will get into your intellect or mindset, and this is the part of us that determines our inner qualities.

> "SHOOT FOR THE MOON, AND IF YOU DON'T HIT THE MOON, YOU MIGHT END UP IN THE STARS."

Inner qualities are the best parameters to determine what you are capable of.

It is not always that you should have one goal. You can have as many as you'd like as long as you have what it takes to achieve them. Les Brown would say, "Shoot for the moon, and if you don't hit the moon, you might end up in the stars." Have you ever heard of BOGO? It means "buy one get one." Simply said, you get two for the price of one. You have one life, but you can simultaneously accomplish different goals in that same life. That's BOGO! Remember Bo Jackson? He was the first professional athlete to become named an "All-Star" in both baseball and football. He excelled in multiple sports, all in one life. That's BOGO! Look at Deion Sanders, how he also excelled in different sporting activities. That shows that you can also do it. If you have the talent, why not go for it?

Many people will tell you to focus your attention on one thing at a time. However, they are just projecting their own limitations and inabilities to multitask at the level you can. So, if you are multitalented, go for it! What do you have to lose? Instead think of what you have to gain.

## HOW TO ACHIEVE YOUR VISION

The vision you have usually impacts others as well as yourself. For example, your major goal could be to help other people to overcome their fear, but you also get more experienced, confident, and satisfied in the process. Now that you know what you want your goals to be within the next one, three, five, or more years, what do you need to make this work and where do you start? An ambition without a plan is simply a dream. It's good to dream, but it is more important to turn your dreams into reality. In this section, I will give you some tips that you could consider in your endeavors to achieve your ambitions.

> IT'S GOOD TO DREAM, BUT IT IS MORE IMPORTANT TO TURN YOUR DREAMS INTO REALITY.

## FOCUS MORE ON THE "WHY" THAN THE "WHAT"

The "why" question defines your purpose more than the "what." Instead of thinking about what you should do, focus on why you would need to do whatever it is that you want to do. Asking "why" helps you to identify problems that you need to solve. What is the purpose of an ambition if it does not address and give solutions to existing problems? Identify an inconvenience that exists in the world. This could be something that doesn't exist today or an improvement of something that already exists. It could also be something that you experienced, heard from the news, or were told by a friend. There could be many problems that you could come across that need to be solved, but focus on what you would love to solve; something that aligns with your passion.

While it is more likely that you will begin to think about your personal fortunes, it is important to align to your purpose when you focus on the bigger picture which includes other people. When the reasons as to why you want to solve the problem involve helping other people, that will be your major motivation even when your initial excitement shrinks or completely falls off. Therefore, when you set your ambitions in place, it is important that you focus on why you want to pursue the ambition.

Let's look at the following ambitions:

- "I want to be a focused Human Resources (HR) Manager."
- "I want to engage with people and improve how they are organized and treated in the health sector."

The first ambition is less explanatory and vague. It sounds like the main focus is on the title. The second one is an answer to the "why" question. It explains the reasons why one wants to pursue the ambition of being an HR manager. It gives the purpose of the ambition which is to "engage with people and improve how they are organized." This is what will keep you going in the event that your ambition faces the tests of circumstances because you will derive your motivation from these reasons (Reader, 2017).

## KEEP YOUR AMBITIONS TO YOURSELF

I know you are wondering why you should keep your ambition to yourself, because we have always been told that the strength to achieve your goals is in speaking out. Therefore, whenever we have a brilliant idea that could develop into an ambition, it is intuitive that we feel the urge to tell someone about it. In 2020, Derek Sivers presented vast research results that stretched back to as far as the 1920s which supported the notion that people who talk about their ambitions are less likely to achieve them (Siver, 2010). You could then say, "I know of people who talked about their ambitions and made it big" or "I talk about my ambitions often and everything tends to work out well." That could be true, but maybe you could have done even better if you had kept your ambition to yourself.

According to Sivers, most of the evidence shows that when you say something that you intend to do before doing it, your mind is tricked into thinking that you have done it already. Usually, achieving your ambitions gives you the gratification and satisfaction that you have done well. This is exactly how you feel when you tell your friends about your ambitions and they support, and even "drink to it" in celebration. Unfortunately, the mind cannot distinguish between imagined and real scenarios, so it responds to both of them in the same way. Once you begin to feel like you have already achieved your goals, then your motivation is compromised. Therefore, let the noise come from your actions.

## PUT EVERYTHING INTO PLACE

When you have your vision in place, the next thing would be to make it happen. Write down all of the things that you need to do to achieve your vision. It is fine if you write them randomly as they come through your mind, but you will need to reorganize them into actionable steps in the preferred order. As you go through these steps and towards your overall ambition, you could tick them off as you accomplish them. This can keep you motivated.

## THE TIME MATRIX

In 2019, I developed a methodology and framework called "The TIME Matrix." TIME stands for "This Is ME." It was originally designed for students to determine what they want to do when they leave school, but I discovered that many adults never really put much thought into their purpose and personal fulfillment.

The procedure for the exercise begins with the students drawing four quadrants. To do this, you take a sheet of paper and place it down horizontally. From the top middle of the page, draw a line from the top to the bottom before drawing another line from the left-hand side to the right-hand side of the page. You should end up with four even boxes. In the box on the top left-hand corner write, "What I Don't Want." In the top right box, write "What I Do Want." In the bottom left box, write "My Superpowers," and then in the bottom right box, write "This Time Next Year."

Begin to fill in the boxes with information. List what you don't want and what you want in your life, career, and relationships according to the labels in the boxes. Go on to identify your superpowers, gifts, and strengths in order to determine what you do extremely well and write these in the "My Superpowers" box. This propels you to the next level, helping you to get what you want in life. "This Time Next Year," allows you to hit your goals or get what you want within a year's time.

I did this exercise for myself in 2019 in preparation for 2020 (see diagram on the next page) and I achieved four out of five things that I wanted. The only thing that

# TIME MATRIX

*Discover Your Other Self*

## What I **DON'T** Want

- I don't want to work for a company that doesn't align with my values
- I don't want a bad boss
- I don't want to work on meaningless tasks
- I don't want to live a boring life

## What I **WANT**

- I want a Tesla by 2022
- I want to work for a company that has remote working capabilities
- I want a boss that allows me to create
- I want to travel to a different country 2 times per year
- I want to make an impact on other peoples lives

## My Super Power (Gifts/Talents)

- I'm an awesome writer
- Kick a$$ presenter
- I lead people to VICTORY!!!
- I easily connect with people
- People ALWAYS come to me for advice
- I manufacture ideas!

## This Time Next Year...

- Facilitate 5 workshops at Universities & Colleges
- I would have travelled to Brazil and Amsterdam
- Working in my field for a company that allows me to work from home
- Grow my LinkedIn Network by 30%
- Create my own podcast

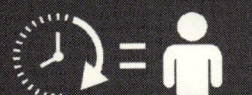

**TIME = This Is ME**

I couldn't achieve was traveling, and that was a result of COVID-19 implications on travel bans.

## DANIEL JOSEPH'S STORY

When we talk about dreams, what usually comes to our minds are visions that we put into place while we are fully conscious without much contribution from the subconscious mind. Here is a man whose day visions and night dreams go hand in hand. Daniel Joseph is the man who has seen the manifestation of his night dreams in reality. No wonder he is called the Dreamcatcher. Does this man's name have anything to do with his successful life? In the Bible, Daniel was a figure who was known for interpreting the Babylonian king's dreams. On the other hand, Joseph from the Bible was a dreamer and an interpreter as well.

Daniel poses dreams as another way of tapping into our other selves. Daniel's passion was in the music and film industry which can be explained by his abilities as a rapper, even at the age of ten. His father noticed this and bought a camera for him, so he started filming at a very young age. Daniel did about 50 films in which he got people in his neighborhood to participate. He had pictures of hip-hop singers all over his room on the ceiling and walls. His passions were evident all over, and this is how he visualized what he wanted to be.

Daniel's interest in dreams arose through psychology classes during his college years. He then decided to embark on a two-year experiment that was aimed at investigating the effects of drugs and alcohol on the ability to remember

## DISCOVER YOUR OTHER SELF

dreams. When he would not remember his dreams, he would document that as part of the results. Daniel also analyzed his dreams in relation to what would have happened during the day. Let's say he would have listened to Eminem's new song during the day, and then at night, he would have a dream about himself, Eminem, and Dr. Dre singing together. He would then deduce that day's activities may have an influence on the dreams that one experiences during the night.

In one of his dreams, Daniel was with Canibus, his favorite rapper. Daniel said, "We were discussing issues about rap and the nature of hip-hop. We discussed how there had been a regression instead of a revolution." In real life, Daniel reached out to Canibus about doing a song together. One thing led to another and the two did a song called "Dreamcatcher" together. In December 2010, Daniel did a show with Canibus. The next day, it was Canibus' birthday and Daniel had the privilege and honor to take his favorite rapper out for a treat. There they were, sitting down and discussing things about hip-hop. This was a dream come true!

> **SILENCE IS A BRIDGE TO THE INFINITE. DANIEL SEES DREAMS AS THAT SILENCE BECAUSE YOU CAN ONLY DREAM WHEN YOU QUIET THE MIND.**

*"Dreams are a great tool if you know how to use them."*

Silence is a bridge to the infinite. Daniel sees dreams as that silence because you can only dream when you quiet the mind. He says, "You know, we are like a river. Up there, it is active and turbulent, but when you go deeper into the riverbed, it is quiet. That is where you are able to explore the horizons of your potential and the depth of your soul."

## LIFE TIPS

1. Why is it good to remember dreams? They are an extension of your soul, subconscious mind, and intentions.
2. Evidence that you are living your dream is deja vu. If you were able to live that dream, then why would you doubt the dreams that are related to the accomplishment of your passions?
3. What you see in your dreams is a reflection of what you can do.
4. Create vision boards - one for your personal life and another for your professional life.
5. Learn the art of writing down your goals.
6. Embrace the rejections because it is from them that you will reap acceptance.

## ACTIVITY

This is an activity that you can do if you want to follow up on your dreams.

1. Get your phone or pen and paper on your bedside before you sleep.
2. Say some positive affirmations before you sleep. You could say, "I am going to remember my dreams."
3. Avoid drugs, alcohol, and smoking because they reduce your ability to go into rapid eye movement (R.E.M.) sleep where you are able to experience more robust dreams.
4. Sleep where you are able to experience more robust dreams.
5. Jot your dreams down within the first 30 seconds after waking up. The longer you procrastinate, the more difficult it becomes to remember the dreams.

## MELANIE ROUSSEAU'S STORY

One of the statements that Melanie Rousseau explained when I interviewed her was, "We had always wanted our own house, but we kept dreaming." In her story, Melanie presents the other type of "dreaming" that most of us are familiar with. Melanie is a mother of two who made a decision to re-invent herself after her second marital separation. Melanie grew and survived in environments where she was always told that she needed to change, and that became an echo that haunted her all the time. She always thought, "I can never be successful if I remain the way that I am." Melanie recalls the moments when she had to be kicked under the table so that she would stop talking. In other words, she was being asked to stop being herself.

During her childhood, her parents always compared her to her brother who was seen as a genius because he had precise answers as to what he wanted to be. Melanie on the other hand would simply say, "I just want to help people," and it was difficult to translate how she was going to help people. Sometimes she would say that she wanted to be a nurse and then her mother would remind her that she needed good grades to be a nurse which was not easy for her to attain.

Melanie had to leave home at the age of 16. She then proceeded to put herself through school and work two jobs so that she could fend for herself. Melanie recalls a point when she was in a relationship that made her cry frequently. All the odds were against her; she was suffering financially, emotionally and physically. One day, she was crying in the bathroom when her seven-year-old son came in and asked her why she was always sad. Like any other mother, Melanie tried to hide her sorrow from her son, but the boy insisted. She then decided to talk to her son using an analogy, and she said, "Sometimes in life, things happen and we let people put us in a cocoon. So, baby, Mom has been in a cocoon for a little while, but now I am deciding that I am going to nibble that hole. At the end of the story, baby, Mom is going to be the beautiful butterfly who is going to be free."

After her second marriage failed, Melanie hit rock bottom as she had no idea where she and her two children were going to stay. After finally finding a place to stay, sleeping on the floor and having no furniture, Melanie discovered her other self and decided to take action. It was through the difficult experiences and the decision to redirect her dreams that gave her the strength to create Money Mama. As time went on, life just started to bring better things into Melanie's life, and now, the sky's the limit. She uses her business to empower other women entrepreneurs and aspiring entrepreneurs to win at business.

> "SOMETIMES IN LIFE, THINGS HAPPEN AND WE LET PEOPLE PUT US IN A COCOON."

## CHAPTER 6: THE TURN-AROUND

WHEN IT RAINS IT POURS. I got two job offers. One of them would have brought me back to my comfort zone, which was the telecommunications industry. While the other would be my first time entering the world of online dating. However, this was not your typical "online dating" service, it was one for married people, Ashley Madison. The telecommunications job would have been easy to fall back into because I knew telecommunications like the back of my hand, but the Ashley Madison job paid more and it would bring me back to the salary that I would have received if that job opportunity that I lost had worked out.

Money was one thing, but my morals came into question. I asked myself, "How can I be part of a service that promotes couples cheating?" I even had a hard time telling my mom because she is a hardcore Catholic and would probably look down at me. Surprisingly, when I told her about the opportunity, she said, "Well, with or without this service, people are going to cheat on their spouses anyway." I took her answer as acceptance, weighed the pros

## DISCOVER YOUR OTHER SELF

and cons, and I was convinced that taking this job would be a stepping stone to something greater.

I decided to take the job at Ashley Madison, but before I started, I had to treat myself to a solo vacation in the Dominican Republic (DR). A few weeks before the vacation, I received calls from two other job opportunities. One of the opportunities was 12 minutes from my house and the other was at a well-known and prestigious athletic wear company, Adidas. The one that was 12 minutes away from my house sounded like a dream come true because I've always had to commute for at least an hour for my other jobs in the past. Working close to home was an ideal situation for me. I responded to the job that was 12 minutes away by telling them that I was going on a vacation and this prompted them to speed up the paperwork to the point that they gave me an offer the day before I left for DR. I told them that I would review the job offer and that I would be available to have further conversations while in DR.

When I was in my hotel room in DR, I decided to be bold in my negotiations because I knew my worth and the value that I could deliver for the company. The company decided to align with my demands, but they had to do some background checks, and this would take another week. The whole scenario put me in a very awkward position because it meant that I had to report to work at Ashley Madison. I had nothing to be worried about in the background check, but I was just in a situation where I left one job for the next, and I didn't want to find myself unemployed again. With that in mind, I made another bold decision to go to Ashley Madison while I awaited the results of my background check. My first and only week there was very eye-opening.

I was used to seeing highly professional presentations and material, yet this time around I was seeing pictures that contained nudity as they would promote their services on selected porn sites. Again, this culture and environment wasn't for me, but I knew this was a stepping stone. By my fourth day at Ashley Madison, I received a notification from the other company informing me that my background checks were complete and I was in the clear! I handed in my resignation to Ashley Madison the next day.

## RESILIENCE IS KEY

There is a point in life where your ability to contain a difficult and challenging situation ends. There is a line that you feel you cannot cross. You might have had some experience with that moment where you feel like giving up and you tell yourself that you've tried your best. In such moments, it is normal to feel that you are vulnerable to fate and the decision that you make at this point depends on you. Remember, there are two types of you - the one that accepts things as they are and is vulnerable to fate and the other is the one that is resilient and determined to go against the rules of fate. The one that does not accept fate is the one that we are calling your other self. If you choose to use the former, you are ready to let your situation defeat you, but when you choose the latter, you are ready to manipulate the difficult situation to your advantage.

There is a thin line between your success and failure, and this line is defined by your decision to trigger your other self into action. In this chapter, you will realize that unless you come across challenges in your life, it is difficult to trigger your other self because challenges are opportunities for growth.

One of the things that you achieve by going through challenges is resilience. Resilience is the mental reservoir for strength that enables you to go through hardships and associated negative emotions without breaking down (Cherry, 2020). Resilience is what marks the differences in response to situations among different people. For example, if a certain disaster appears, there are some people who seem to remain calm, less stressed, and tend to comfort other people who are in the same situation as them. You might be familiar with similar situations where some people seem to be okay in overwhelming circumstances. This is resilience, and some people are born with it, but the most powerful resilience is created and maintained through life.

> **RESILIENCE IS THE MENTAL RESERVOIR FOR STRENGTH THAT ENABLES YOU TO GO THROUGH HARDSHIPS AND ASSOCIATED NEGATIVE EMOTIONS WITHOUT BREAKING DOWN.**

Resilience does not stop difficulties and challenges from coming. It also does not stop individuals from experiencing the emotions that are associated with life's challenges. Even the most resilient individuals feel the pain of losing loved ones. The difference is that they are able to go through the emotions and recover quicker than their non-resilient counterparts. Non-resilient individuals' dwell in the effects of life's challenges for longer and usually exhibit emotions such as regret, blame, and bitterness.

Everyone has some level of resilience in them, but not all resistance can take you through the difficult moments of life. There are two forms of resilience. Inherent resilience is the one that we are born with. It is essential for survival as it can help you to go through your day-to-day activities. This is the natural resilience that helps us to explore the world, try new things, and take some risks in life.

There is another form of resilience that develops due to difficult encounters in life. This is called adapted resilience. This type of resilience is created. For example, going through break-ups or divorce are challenges that create adapted resilience. There is also resilience that develops over time based on difficult events and circumstances that we go through. This is referred to as learned resilience and it is the strength that you can borrow from your past experiences to help you cope with stress, anxiety, and other emotions that are associated with difficult situations. Learned resilience helps us to learn, grow and develop our mechanisms for managing stressful situations and identify ways to draw strength that we did not know we had during the times when it became a tool for survival (Miles, 2015).

## JEROME SAMUELS' STORY

Jerome Samuels is one of the people that I interviewed on the DYOS show, and the major theme that characterized this session was Jerome's resilience. Jerome described resilience as a "mental muscle" that helps your brain to cope with difficult situations.

At the age of 15, Jerome started to have anxiety attacks which became a thorn in his side. The attacks were so severe that he wouldn't be able to go back home from school on his own and his parents would have to go and pick him up. Symptoms of anxiety attacks include overwhelming fear, sweating, trembling, chest pain, and palpitations. This is what Jerome was going through every now and then. At that time, he began to believe that this was his way of life until one day, his mother raised the idea that he needed to accept that things were going to change. She taught him not to bury himself in the challenges of today, but to prepare for a different tomorrow. That marked the development of resilience in Jerome's life.

> SHE TAUGHT HIM NOT TO BURY HIMSELF IN THE CHALLENGES OF TODAY, BUT TO PREPARE FOR A DIFFERENT TOMORROW.

Here are some of the things that Jerome learned as he put resilience into practice in his own life:

- Master your mind and learn to control it.
- Do not spend time worrying about the things that you cannot change even if you want to. Instead, focus on what you can do to affect change.
- Set goals that are time related, and work towards them.

- Achieve your goals in your mind before you can achieve them in real time.
- Doubt will often seep through your mind, but develop ways to shut it off.

Being resilient is not for the faint of heart. While we all have inherent resilience, we still need to adopt ways of developing learned and adapted resilience which is more powerful in coping with difficult situations.

## THE ART OF BUILDING RESILIENCE

**Direct your thoughts toward positivity:** This does not imply that you should look at situations unrealistically and paint everything the same color. You should learn to look at situations that are negative in a way that neither accommodates blame nor worrying over things that you cannot change. This technique helps you to identify opportunities that are hidden in challenges so that you are able to see the positive side of the challenge.

**Talk to someone:** When you have a challenge and you talk to someone that you trust, the challenge will not go away, but it will make you feel like it's shared, and therefore, you will feel lighter. Besides, two heads are better than one. You can get more ideas on how to deal with a difficult situation from others who probably went through something similar as you. This gives you what I call "borrowed resilience." For example, a person who has had multiple miscarriages can strengthen someone who just had their first miscarriage.

**Attend to yourself:** Sometimes we get so caught up in

our busy schedules to an extent that we forget to take care of ourselves. Eating healthy food, getting enough sleep, keeping yourself hydrated, and getting enough exercise are important considerations that can keep you physically and mentally healthy. This is important in building resilience. Techniques such as meditation are also effective in training your mind to cope with stress and anxiety that comes with difficult situations of life.

## PASSING OVER OPPORTUNITIES REPEATEDLY (POOR)

I recall an old friend of mine by the name of Raymond Kingu Jr, defining the word "poor" as an acronym that represents **P**assing **O**ver **O**pportunities **R**epeatedly. This definition is interesting because it is different from the perceptions that most of us have on poverty. Unlike other definitions that focus on "lack," this definition represents the major cause of poverty found within your mind.

It is unfortunate that when challenges come, even natural disasters like the COVID-19 pandemic, most people tend to concentrate on the bad side of the story. If you focus on the loss of jobs, deteriorating health, or rising mortality rates, that is what you will see. This does not mean that you shouldn't follow news updates about what is happening, but the problem comes when you take it to heart and consider that as what is happening everywhere. It could be happening, but there are some people who are referring to those problems as opportunities. I know that this may sound a bit awkward, but truly speaking, there are some people who are grateful that the COVID-19 came because to them, it presented an opportunity for growth. That is why there are always people who make it big during national and international crises when everyone else would have lost hope.

> **IT IS ONE THING TO SEE OPPORTUNITIES AND IT IS ANOTHER TO SEIZE THEM,**

Opportunities always present themselves, and there is no doubt that you missed a lot of opportunities to grow in your life. What we do when we see these opportunities is what defines whether we shrink and get poor or we grow and get wealthier. No matter what we go through, the ability to identify opportunities and seize them is crucial. It is one thing to see opportunities and it is another to seize them, but both of these concepts are important tools in creating a growth mindset and a turnaround in your life. Let's explore more about the POOR concept in this section.

## IDENTIFYING OPPORTUNITIES

Even before the pandemic, adversities have always been part of our lives. However, COVID-19 added to our adversities. While it is only natural that we feel the pain, mourn, regret, and succumb to stress and anxiety, there must come a time when we have to move on with our lives. There are two ways through which we can derive opportunities during the course of adversity. You can either look for opportunities that are embedded within the adversity or you can turn the adversity into an opportunity.

## DISCOVER YOUR OTHER SELF

# OPPORTUNITIES CREATED THROUGH ADVERSITIES

Challenges and adversities can present great opportunities for success. It is important that we learn to quickly identify opportunities before they are seized by others. Whether we like it or not, we are competing for the same opportunities with others, so if you do not identify them, someone else will. Nelson Mandela once said, "I do not lose. I either win or learn" (Laux, 2017). If you can't succeed from adversity, you can at least learn from it. Either way, you would have taken adversity as an opportunity.

> **"I DO NOT LOSE. I EITHER WIN OR LEARN"**

1. **Analyze:** Investigate all aspects around adversity. Find answers to questions like, "How did it start?" "How did you feel as a result of the adversity?" or "Is there anything that I can do to reduce or alleviate the effects of adversity?" Businesses are based on efforts to solve the problems that people face, and answers to questions such as the ones above can be great ideas for businesses, as long as someone is willing to pay for it.

2. **Address your thoughts, perceptions, and attitude:** Whatever has happened must have caused some negative perceptions, emotions, and attitudes. I do not recommend that you shun them and act as if nothing happened. Acknowledge them, but do whatever you can to move on. Focus on the fact that whatever you went through was a learning experience,

and through it, you have gained more experience, strength, wisdom, and resilience. Be energized by the fact that adversities are opportunities for growth.

Some say, "Attitude is everything," and I can't say it any better. Attitudes are a reflection of the way you think because thoughts become perception, and perceptions sprout into attitudes. Your attitude determines how you relate with others, how others perceive you, whether you react to situations or are proactive, and how you view situations of life. If you tame your thoughts and direct them towards positivity, you will develop a positive attitude that makes it easy for you to identify opportunities even in the biggest adversities. Mindfulness techniques such as meditation are great ways of nurturing positivity in your mind.

## TURNING ADVERSITIES INTO OPPORTUNITIES

Turning adversities into opportunities is an art that you can learn over time, and it is based on creating a positive mindset.

1. **Focus on the good things:** Everything that happens on this earth has its advantages and disadvantages, depending on how you look at it. Instead of concentrating on the adverse side of the situation, you could choose to focus on the good side and define the situation that way. For example, the coronavirus brought a lot of negative effects like pain, death, and alterations to face-to-face social interactions.

You could choose to focus on the fact that the pandemic gave you the chance to have more time with your family or you could see it as a vehicle to the long-awaited digitalization. Therefore, everything is defined according to how you see it.

> **EVERYTHING IS DEFINED ACCORDING TO HOW YOU SEE IT.**

2. **Focus on your capabilities:** Take the adversity as an opportunity to show what you've got. Perceive it as a chance to put into practice what you learned from previous encounters with life's challenges.

3. **Adopt an Illusionist Mindset:** Create your own reality. Think about David Blaine or Harry Houdini. These two illusionists created their own version of reality. You can do the same with your life by envisioning and manifesting your desires into reality. This is a mind hack that requires you to rewire your brain through daily affirmations and conversations you have with yourself to achieve anything you set your intentions on.

## SEIZING OPPORTUNITIES

Identifying opportunities is not the same as seizing them. While some people fail in life because they were unable to see opportunities, some fail because they saw the opportunities but did not seize them. What attitude do you need for you to successfully seize opportunities?

**Authenticate yourself:** Honestly define who you are and

> "PASSION IS ENERGY. FEEL THE POWER THAT COMES FROM FOCUSING ON WHAT EXCITES YOU."

what you love. What do you do best and what are the capabilities of your other self? It doesn't matter how many opportunities you see; wisdom and maturity will teach you that not all of them are meant for you. If an opportunity arises that triggers your inner being and interest, then go for it. Attempting to seize the wrong opportunity is as good as failing to seize the right opportunity. Oprah Winfrey said, "Passion is energy. Feel the power that comes from focusing on what excites you."

**Be clear on your purpose:** Every one of us has a purpose that we should fulfill. This purpose is unique to you and is closely associated with the true authentication of who you are. Your purpose in life should tally with the goals that you set. Therefore, you should seize opportunities that are aligned with your goals and purpose. This helps you to increase your chances of success in your endeavors.

**Don't list giving up among your options:** Successful people are not people who never failed, but rather they are people who refused to give up even when they failed many times. If you find an opportunity and you try to monetize it, don't expect everything to go smoothly, but don't give up either. Remember, it's not failure, it's either you win or you learn. Reinforce that mindset and you will have no room for regret.

DISCOVER YOUR OTHER SELF

# SARA NATHANSON'S STORY

Sara Nathanson is the only non-lawyer sibling in a family of five kids. Being the Vice President of Talent at Aritzia (a premium fashion company), Sarah had a lot of insights when it comes to seizing opportunities that are quite beneficial:

- Run towards the fire. Always be willing to run towards the problem with the aim to help solve it. Don't walk past a problem. If you see it, you are accountable for it, so you must take responsibility.
- Be willing to solve problems, not to create them.
- You should know what you are looking for while being open to what you find.
- When you open up to your connections about the opportunities that you are looking for, be specific about what you want. Many people want to support you, but when you present a lot of unorganized information, it's more stressful to go through. Being specific and putting your information in a digestible manner makes it easier for you to get help. Simply said, make it easy for someone to help you.
- There are four questions that you should ask when you are looking for a job.

    1. What do I want to do?
    2. Where do I want to work?
    3. With whom do I want to work with and for?
    4. How much money do I want to earn?

It is interesting to note that the answers to these questions are the ones that helped me to decide on which job I would take. This shows how practical Sara's ideas are. Use them and you will be on the right track.

## CHAPTER 7:
### YOU TOO CAN SURVIVE

In March 2019, I bumped into Cara McCarron, an old tenant of mine, at Walmart. Remember the house I purchased to be closer to kids, but I couldn't move into because the mother of my children took me to court? Cara was the tenant that occupied that very same house until I was financially stable to manage all my financial obligations.

When I arrived at Walmart, Cara had just parked her car right beside mine. I tried to avoid her at first because I didn't want to talk to her or see anyone during this time. I knew she would ask me how everything was going and I didn't want to tell her about my makeshift cast for my broken hand and unemployment status. I looked like a mess, so I pretended like I didn't see her park beside me. I let her go into Walmart with her daughter before I followed. As I was doing my grocery shopping, I heard an excited voice saying, "Reggie! Is that you?" I turned around anxiously and I said, "Oh, hi Cara. How are you?" We talked for about three minutes to sum up our current state of affairs. She then asked me if I would be open to going with her for coffee. I had nothing else to do, so I obliged.

Cara and I went for coffee the following week. She asked me if I knew Tony Robbins. I told her that I had heard of him but never had the opportunity to listen to or watch his content. She then asked me if I wanted to attend one of his conferences in Dallas, Texas. Something told me to say, "Yes," even though I still had no job and was supposed to be managing my money accordingly.

In July of that same year, I went to the Tony Robbins conference with Cara and her friends. When I first got to the conference I thought, *what cult is this?* as people were hugging as well as giving each other massages and high-fives. The arena was cold, but I later found out that it was by design and was meant to keep people awake. It was a four-day event, and one of the most memorable moments that changed my life was a segment that they call "Transformation Day." This is where Tony takes you on a deep meditation to release all your past hurts. The arena was pitch black and as he took the audience through the exercise, I could hear people releasing their pain. When I say releasing the pain, I mean you would hear people screaming. It even prompted me to scream also so that I could release everything that had been holding me back. From that day forward, I was transformed and I felt like I could tackle the world.

Discovering your other self is one thing, but staying motivated is another. Most of our efforts to conquer difficult times and to be successful in life depends on the extent to which we are motivated. Creating and sustaining momentum can be difficult even under the best circumstances. Imagine trying to stay motivated when you have lost all family members to the COVID-19 pandemic, you are sick, your job is gone, and you can't even call a friend to give you encouragement. In my case it was loss of a relationship, losing over $20,000 to court cases in an effort to have more time with my kids, being completely shut out of my children's lives, losing my job, and the uncertainty of the future.

Despite the difficulties, I did survive. Many other people like Timothy Mutto, Veronica Owusu, Melanie Rousseau, Brian Schulman, and Glenn Lundy survived the storms in their lives. I am certain that you can survive it too. I have dedicated this chapter to exploring how to create and sustain motivation and positivity that will give you the strength to pull through adversities and look into the future with confidence.

## THE LAW OF ATTRACTION

The Law of Attraction states that "like attracts like." This law is based on the philosophy that positive thoughts pull positive things into your life while the negative ones bring negative outcomes (Scott, 2007). The secret behind the Law of Attraction is that you should focus on positive things for you to receive good things in your life. The Law of Attraction is not a form of magic that mysteriously brings things into existence. It is a philosophy that supports

> **POSITIVE THOUGHTS PULL POSITIVE THINGS INTO YOUR LIFE WHILE THE NEGATIVE ONES BRING NEGATIVE OUTCOMES**

the notion that what you spend your time thinking and believing will eventually materialize.

"Thoughts become things" is a saying that describes the concept of the Law of Attraction. Each thought is made up of energy and is characterized by its own frequency which is unique to itself. The energy and frequency of one thought radiates out into the universe, and when it does, it interacts with the material world. The well-established concept of quantum mechanics presents the fact that all matter, including physical objects, are packets of energy at the sub-microscopic quantum level. Therefore, as your thought radiates into the universe, it attracts things that have the same energy and frequency as itself. This implies that it attracts like objects, thoughts, and people, and these are the things that will materialize in your life.

Unfortunately, we don't choose whether we want the Law of Attraction to affect us. It simply does. What happens is that in everything that we do, thoughts are involved. In each case they are either positive or negative - nothing in between. So, even when you are not aware, positive thought will eventually materialize as positive outcomes while the same applies to negative thoughts. It is important that you learn to stay positive all the time as this will ensure that you are pulling positivity towards you.

## THE POWER OF YOUR MOUTH

Christians believe in the power of the mouth, a concept which goes hand in hand with the Law of Attraction. The Bible says, "Death and life are in the power of the tongue, and those who love it will eat its fruit," (Proverbs 18:21). This verse implies that the tongue has the power to bring things into being through words. Words create things, so whatever you say is what happens. It is crucial to understand this concept and apply it for your own good and the good of others. It can help to frame negative situations in a positive way. With words, you can call success, good health, wisdom, strength to conquer adversities, and opportunities into existence.

> "DEATH AND LIFE ARE IN THE POWER OF THE TONGUE, AND THOSE WHO LOVE IT WILL EAT ITS FRUIT,"

## BUILD POSITIVE CONNECTIONS

Our interactions have to do with our success or failure. Surround yourself with people who have positive mindsets. I believe that positivity is contagious, but so is negativity. Spending time with people who speak positively will help you to grow more positive. Suppose you are stuck on the phone with someone who is constantly speaking negatively. You can just excuse yourself by telling the other person that you have other commitments.

It can be easier to just let everyone know that you do not accommodate consistent nonproductive "negative talks." Consuming a constant negative worldview can impact negatively on your mental and even physical state, so your connections should ideally be overall positive influences that support one another.

## CELEBRATE ACCOMPLISHMENTS

Whether your accomplishment is big or small, develop

a culture of celebrating them. Positivity is evident in appreciating every effort that brought about, even the smallest achievement. Appreciate yourself for the efforts, the sleepless nights, the sacrifices, the tears and smiles that collaboratively contributed to your accomplishment. Go out for an ice cream or consider treating yourself with a special movie night. There is no harm in rewarding yourself for what you have achieved. Give yourself a shout-out, you are worth it. Be sure to celebrate not too long after the accomplishment.

## READ INSPIRING CONTENT

Digitalization came with infinite information. Both harmful and harmless information is available in abundance on the internet. Be selective of the information that you read because when you read, you feed your mind with the positivity or negativity which is embedded in the information that you read. I would recommend that you read stories and testimonies of people who are positive.

## JOHNNY EARLE'S STORY

This is a man who believes in the power of positivity in doing things differently, and he lives up to it. By the time he turned 16, Johnny Earle had started 16 businesses through which he learned much of the skills that he currently applies to his successful business. He was a Disc Jockey (DJ) and did magic tricks at parties. If I have ever seen a man who

## DISCOVER YOUR OTHER SELF

talks about failure like it's a piece of cake, Johnny is the one.

Johnny owns a T-shirt bakery and operates under the trade name "Johnny Cupcakes." His "bakery" doesn't contain food. Instead, there are T-shirts displayed in the refrigerators, and the T-shirts are packaged in

> "I WENT FROM DOING MAGIC TRICKS AT BIRTHDAY PARTIES TO DOING MAGIC WITH THE BRAND."

pastry boxes. This is how he creates memorable experiences for his customers and keeps them begging for more. "It's like I went from doing magic tricks at birthday parties to doing magic with the brand," according to Johnny. Now, Johnny has opened over 1,000 pop-up shops all over the world in collaboration with the likes of Teenage Mutant Ninja Turtles and The Simpsons in order to create unique and memorable experiences for his customer base. As of now, Johnny is known for helping other people to create blueprints that help them to build brand loyalty.

## LIFE TIPS

There are a number of positivity tips that you can derive from Johnny. Here are some of them:

1. Good packaging does not get thrown away. It acts as a miniature billboard.
2. I have been able to fail and fail fast which has eventually led me to find my passion.

3. Don't just collect connections, but figure out ways to make those connections work.
4. When you do things differently, people will talk about them.
5. Giving back is a good way to say thank you to your customers and it builds brand loyalty.

# CHAPTER 8:
## BUILDING NEW MUSCLES

At this point, Dameon Wilson's words made sense to me. The other version of myself that had been lying idle all along had been awakened and was beginning to show off. I began to do some things that I had never dreamed of doing. This came as a result of the quest to find out more truth and answers to the question, "Who am I?" Losing my job turned out to be a blessing in disguise. I doubt that I was ever going to develop the guts to build new muscles and a mindset that has helped propel my career and life to new levels. This point in time also reminds me of the Bible passage my mom often quoted me when I was going through these dark moments, Genesis 50:20, "What you intended against me for evil, God intended for good, in order to accomplish a day like this— to preserve the lives of many people." This was speaking to my former employers that took it upon

> "WHAT YOU INTENDED AGAINST ME FOR EVIL, GOD INTENDED FOR GOOD."

themselves to interfere with my future employment. If it wasn't for them, I wouldn't be writing this book.

Further to this, I constructed and outlined requirement documents and then developed a minimal viable product (MVP) to build a web application that will revolutionize the job application process. This application would make it super easy for employers to recruit talent and for job seekers to apply for jobs. I also decided to create my own personal branding company by providing marketing and branding support to individuals and businesses that are looking to increase awareness and drive impressions. This momentum that I was building led me to develop a series of workshops called, "Design Your X-Factor". These workshops are designed to help students across the globe successfully transition into the real world. Facilitating these workshops created the foundation I needed to create DYOS, which is a virtual community that aims to inspire and change lives for the better.

Last but not least, I started to take up acting and have appeared in multiple TV commercials. Now imagine if I didn't lose my job, I would have just been going through the motions of life without realizing all of the opportunities that were in front of me the whole time!

## COVID-19 AND THE QUEST FOR TRUTH

The pandemic swept across the world and a lot of unanswered questions remain outstanding. How did it come into existence? Was it from fish, wild animals, or birds? Is the virus natural or is it a result of genetic manipulations? If the latter is true, then was the manipulation intentional or a mistake? New variants are emerging. What could have caused the emergence of these variants? Could it be climatic conditions or natural mutations? If a mutation is the answer, is it a single or there are multiple mutations?

With the abundance of information that is available on the internet, people now find it difficult to acquaint themselves with the truth. Some information relates the emergence and existence of the coronavirus with political warfare. The pandemic has turned the whole globe into a battlefield as people fight against the spread of the pandemic. All lockdowns were political efforts to combat the spread of the virus. As in any battle, many people have lost their lives while some sustained both physical and emotional injuries.

One of the greatest things that the pandemic brought was the need to question our survival. The crisis brought many to the realization that life is short, and it is very easy to leave this earth without fulfilling our life's purpose. Consider the lockdowns during which people lost their jobs. Some lost their pillars of confidence, loved ones, and connections among other things that they used to define themselves. This then brings us back to Veronica Owusu's question, "After all has been taken away and you are only left with yourself, who are you?"

This became the time when we realized our need for social connection more than ever before. It was the time when we realized how much we have been neglecting our family relationships in pursuit of titles, riches, and livelihood. We began

> **LIFE IS SHORT, AND IT IS VERY EASY TO LEAVE THIS EARTH WITHOUT FULFILLING OUR LIFE'S PURPOSE.**

to question who we are in the eyes of our loved ones and those who invest their time in us. It is good that we might have realized ourselves, but is that enough? We still have the mandate to live up to the person that we would have realized in us. Fulfill your purpose and let the world benefit from your faithfulness to who you are. I discovered my own definition of who I am and I am making all efforts to live up to it. One day all of us will have to answer the question, "What did you do during the pandemic?" How are you going to respond to this question? What did you discover about yourself? What did you do to help and serve others during this time? For your sake I hope you didn't spend majority of your time living life in an anxious state or find yourself watching Netflix all day.

## X-FACTOR WORKSHOPS

I have always wanted to add value to other people's lives and equip them to be the best that they can be, and whenever I do that, I do it with passion. Apart from connecting with people through the DYOS show on LinkedIn Live, I have engaged with multiple Colleges and Universities so that I can teach their students about things that are critical to their success post-graduation that are not covered in their curriculum.

I realized school literature or the average textbook doesn't talk about bad bosses and there are a bunch of them out there. How do we recognize and cope with a hostile, discriminatory, or otherwise harmful workplace environment? I also teach them how to effectively build a network along with other tools that they will require on their career journey to be successful. My aim was to bridge the gap between the theoretical knowledge of what can possibly exist and the reality of what can be expected in the workplace. In other words, I'm teaching them about things that you won't find in your average textbook.

Through this project, I want to provide students with the tools that I was never provided with when I started my career. I look forward to helping students:

- Become well equipped as they enter the workforce
- Manage fierce competition
- Be exceptional leaders
- Be innovative and creative in their approach to help evolve the marketplace

I want to thank the University of Toronto (Scarborough Campus) and Ryerson University for opening their doors, minds, and hearts by giving me a platform to give back to the students the formula that they need to navigate through their career journey. I also want to thank Manjot Bining, Jen Davies, Olga Popova, Maricruz Rodriguez, Paulina Jankowska, and Jennifer Barcelona for supporting an initiative of this nature, and for seeing and believing in my vision.

Most recently, I heard voices that said, "Go Global." This was God telling me that I need to think bigger and get this program on a global scale. As a result, I am preparing to expand this program to Caribbean countries like Martinique and Guadeloupe and to African countries like Cameroon. With obedience comes opportunity! We're going global!

## MY GRATITUDE

In alignment with the wave of being grateful that has become the trademark for starting every DYOS session, I would like to thank the following individuals for helping me during my rock bottom journey:

| | |
|---|---|
| My parents - Myrna and Reginald Waterman | Peter Pejouyan |
| Melissa Waterman | Delisle Murray aka DJ D. Money |
| Christine Peterson | Todd Deware |
| Rula Safieh | Paul Yantus |
| Dameon Wilson | Gerry Malisani |
| Cara McCarron | Barret Van Allen |
| Anthony Sesel | Adjin Agic |
| Nicholas Waddell | Gennike Mayers |
| Loy Sequeira | Sam Wong |
| Leena Marwah | Celine Campbell |
| Grace Jivani | Christine McCabe |
| Francois Gravel | Ashley Truong |
| Sanjay Bakshani | Andy Ramcharan |
| Vicken Kanadjian | Kareem Perez |

I would like to give a special thanks to all of my featured guests on the DYOS show and of course to the amazing DYOS community for continuously showing up!

More gratitude goes to the following people for choosing to be an inspiration to others:

Veronica Owusu                     Daniel Joseph

## DISCOVER YOUR OTHER SELF

Johnny Earle aka
Johnny Cupcakes

Jerome Samuels

Lila Smith

Kristin Sherry

Sara Nathanson

Cabral Richards
aka Cabbie

Jahmaal Marshall

Brian Schulman

Melanie Rousseau

Timothy Muttoo

Glenn Lundy

# CONCLUSION

THIS IS NOT A STORY solely focused on one individual, but it is a story that describes how I discovered my other self and the mission that I am on so that I can help others to tap into their own paths of self-discovery in order to realize victory. My name is Reggie Waterman, the host of a live stream called Discover Your Other Self (DYOS). In this book, I discussed my own hardships and how 2019 was my personal "COVID-19" during which I hit rock bottom.

The events in my life recounted what happened to many people during the COVID-19 pandemic. Some of such things include the following:

- Losing jobs
- Discrimination
- Separation from families

I was also separated from my family during most of the pandemic as the mother of my children made it her mission to keep us apart during this time. I often make a joke where I say that she's been preparing the children for COVID-19 from the time they were born (social distancing from their father). All of the stories and experiences that I captured were a means to create a time capsule for my children so that they can know who their dad is and how I too had to fight through adversities and be an anchor of support for others during the pandemic.

## DISCOVER YOUR OTHER SELF

It is intuitive that when we face adversities, our focus is glued on the negative effects of the challenges that we go through. This book emphasizes the presence of opportunities that are presented within or together with adversities. These opportunities cannot be identified when the focus is solely on negative factors. When we choose to shift our focus towards positivity, we are able to identify more positive opportunities. It is one thing to notice opportunities and it is another to seize them. If either of these two is not done well, then success cannot be guaranteed.

Having gone through it all, I had to battle with emotions of stress, anxiety, fear, and uncertainty. That was the time when I realized that there are two beings in every individual. One operates when things are just fine and the other one operates during challenging scenarios of life. The first is the one that operates most of the time and is not as deeply associated with resilience. The second one is the one that is associated with resilience and operates upon your permission. This is the being that I call the other self.

Suppose that you discover your other self. You need the motivation to maintain positivity that supports your other self. Factors such as accepting things that you cannot change, learning from your mistakes, celebrating accomplishments, reading inspiring information, and building positive and meaningful connections are some of the things that help you to maintain positivity. Good luck on your journey to discovering your greatness, and I hope that my story inspired you along your way.

## I HOPE YOU HAVE ENJOYED

It has been a pleasure and honor to share my story along with the special individuals that were willing to share theirs. May God bless you and help you achieve your greatest desires.

I would love for you to be part of the DYOS community. For more information on upcoming shows and events please visit:

**www.discoveryourotherself.com**

To learn more about my workshops and information on how to build your personal brand visit:

**www.reggiewaterman.com**

# REFERENCES

*5 steps to discover your life's ambition.* (2015, August 5). Bonfire. https://www.bonfireyoga.com.au/events-and-blogs/blog/5-steps-to-discover-your-lifes-ambition/

Agarwal, P. (2018, August 29). *How to create a positive workplace culture.* Forbes. https://www.forbes.com/sites/pragyaagarwaleurope/2018/08/29/how-to-create-a-positive-work-place-culture/?sh=17d426e84272

Bas, D., Martin, M., Pollack, C., & Venne, R. (2020). *The impact of COVID-19 on sport, physical activity and well-being and its effects on social development.* https://www.un.org/development/desa/dspd/wp-content/uploads/sites/22/2020/05/PB_73.pdf

Brenner, G. H. (2020, September 10). *Impact of COVID-19 on relationship conflict and sexuality.* Psychology Today. https://www.psychologytoday.com/za/blog/experimentations/202009/impact-covid-19-relationship-conflict-and-sexuality

Brownwell, T. (2020, October 16). *Divorce rates and COVID-19.* The National Law Review. https://www.natlawreview.com/article/divorce-rates-and-covid-19

Burke, M. (2020). *60 lives, 60 days: Stories of coronavirus victims from across the U.S.* NBC News. https://www.nbcnews.com/news/obituaries/coronavirus-deaths-60-stories-victims-around-country-n1194396

Cherry, K. (2020, September 19). *How resilience helps with the coping of crisis*. Verywell Mind. https://www.verywellmind.com/what-is-resilience-2795059

Cimberle, M. (2020, October 20). *Increased digital screen time during COVID-19 may accelerate myopia epidemic*. www.Healio.com. https://www.healio.com/news/ophthalmology/20201014/increased-digital-screen-time-during-covid19-may-accelerate-myopia-epidemic

Cooper, A. (2015, July 23). *10 online scams that target small businesses*. Howstuffworks. https://money.howstuffworks.com/10-online-scams-that-target-small-businesses.htm

*Diversification of student recruitment markets*. (2020, March 20). Studyportals. https://studyportals.com/blog/diversification-of-student-recruitment-markets/

Editor. (2020, November 12). *"You can see the regret": ICU nurse on patients who failed to take COVID precautions*. News.wbfo.org. https://news.wbfo.org/post/icu-nurse-dealing-latest-coronavirus-outbreak-michigan

Evans, M. L., Lindauer, M., & Farrell, M. E. (2020). A pandemic within a pandemic — Intimate partner violence during Covid-19. *New England Journal of Medicine*. https://doi.org/10.1056/nejmp2024046

The TIME Matrix. Reggie Waterman (2019).

FindLaw's Team. (2017). *Types of domestic violence*. Findlaw. https://family.findlaw.com/domestic-violence/types-of-domestic-violence.html

Gleeson, B. (2020, September 9). *11 ways to turn adversity into opportunity*. Forbes. https://www.forbes.com/sites/brentgleeson/2020/09/09/11-ways-to-turn-adversity-into-opportunity/?sh=67d0ef6e69c1

Hall, S. (2020, April 9). *This is how COVID-19 is affecting the world of sports.* World Economic Forum. https://www.weforum.org/agenda/2020/04/sports-covid19-coronavirus-excersise-specators-media-coverage/

Hormone Health Network. (2018, November). *Cortisol Hormone Health Network.* www.hormone.org. https://www.hormone.org/your-health-and-hormones/glands-and-hormones-a-to-z/hormones/cortisol

Hunter, C. (2014). *The negative effects of unforgiveness on mental health.* Theravive. https://www.theravive.com/today/post/the-negative-effects-of-unforgiveness-on-mental-health-0001467.aspx

Hutchins, E., & Enomoto, K. (2020). *COVID-19 and behavioral health: Consequences for companies and employees.* www.Mckinsey.com. https://www.mckinsey.com/industries/healthcare-systems-and-services/our-insights/covid-19-and-behavioral-health-consequences-for-companies-and-employees

Jones, K. (2020, October 9). *This chart shows just how much COVID-19 has affected mental health in America.* World Economic Forum. https://www.weforum.org/agenda/2020/10/emotion-mental-health-coronavirus-covid-19-pandemic-usa-us-america-chart-stats/

Laux, C. (2017, April 9). *How moments of adversity are your greatest opportunities.* Goalcast. https://www.goalcast.com/2017/04/09/moments-adversity-greatest-opportunities/

*Law of Attraction.* (2018). The Official Website of The Secret. https://www.thesecret.tv/law-of-attraction/

Lipscy, P. Y. (2020). COVID-19 and the politics of crisis. *International Organization*, 1–30. https://doi.org/10.1017/s0020818320000375

Medical Xpress. (2021, January 12). *What we know about South Africa's coronavirus variant*. Medicalxpress.com. https://medicalxpress.com/news/2021-01-south-africa-coronavirus-variant.html

Miles, J. (2015). *The importance of building resilience*. Counselling-UK. https://www.counselling-directory.org.uk/memberarticles/the-importance-of-building-resilience

National Institute on Aging. (2019, April 23). *Social isolation, loneliness in older people pose health risks*. National Institute on Aging. https://www.nia.nih.gov/news/social-isolation-loneliness-older-people-pose-health-risks

New King James Version (NKJV) Bible.

O'Connor, M. (n.d.). *Ten factors that will help you achieve your goals*. O'Connor Executive Search. http://oces.ie/ten-factors-will-help-achieve-goals/

Ouellette, C. (2020, December 11). *Online shopping statistics you need to know in 2020*. OptinMonster. https://optinmonster.com/online-shopping-statistics/

Patel, D. (2018, September 10). *10 ways successful people push through adversity*. Entrepreneur. https://www.entrepreneur.com/article/319357

Peters, J. (2020, October 9). *A beginner's guide to using Zoom*. The Verge. https://www.theverge.com/21506307/zoom-guide-how-to-free-account-register-sign-up-log-in-invite

Pew Research Center. (2020, March 30). *Most Americans say coronavirus outbreak has impacted their lives.* Pew Research Center's Social & Demographic Trends Project. https://www.pewsocialtrends.org/2020/03/30/most-americans-say-coronavirus-outbreak-has-impacted-their-lives/

Pierce, S. (2014, March 12). *10 Ways To Stay Motivated When Negativity Seems To Be All Around.* HuffPost. https://www.huffpost.com/entry/10-ways-to-stay-motivated_b_4941277

Reader, S. (2017, July 4). *How do we achieve our goals, our ambitions and our big life plans?* Medium. https://medium.com/wondr-blog/how-do-we-achieve-our-goals-our-ambitions-our-big-life-plans-5693f11a87ea

Roylab Stats. (2020). Coronavirus pandemic: Real time counter, World Map, News. *YouTube.* https://www.youtube.com/watch?v=NMre6IAAAiU

Santos-Longhurst, A. (2018, August 31). *High cortisol symptoms: What do they mean?* Healthline. https://www.healthline.com/health/high-cortisol-symptoms#symptoms

Savage, M. (2020, December 7). *Why the pandemic is causing spikes in break-ups and divorces.* www.bbc.com. https://www.bbc.com/worklife/article/20201203-why-the-pandemic-is-causing-spikes-in-break-ups-and-divorces

Scott, E. (2007, February 19). *Understanding and using the Law of Attraction in your life.* Verywell Mind. https://www.verywellmind.com/understanding-and-using-the-law-of-attraction-3144808

Sivers, D. (2010). Keep your goals to yourself. *YouTube.* https://www.youtube.com/watch?v=NHopJHSlVo4

Surico, P., & Galeotti, A. (2020). *The economics of a pandemic: The case of Covid-19.* https://www.far.org.nz/assets/files/blog/files/3093ca6a-a676-568f-9e7c-5dc77c4e188f.pdf

van Vugt, T. (2020, March 20). *Diversification of student recruitment markets.* Studyportals. https://studyportals.com/blog/diversification-of-student-recruitment-markets/

Waterman, R. (n.d.). Discover your "Other" self with Jerome Samuels - Resilience is key (Full version). *YouTube.* www.Youtube.com. https://www.youtube.com/watch?v=VDBeT-GJPXU

WebMD. (2016, December 13). *10 tips to manage stress.* WebMD. https://www.webmd.com/balance/guide/tips-to-control-stress

*Week 23 - Forgiveness.* (2019, March 14). The positivity project. https://posproject.org/week-23-forgiveness/

World Health Organization. (2020). *Practical considerations and recommendations for religious leaders and faith-based communities in the context of COVID-19.* https://www.who.int/publications-detail-redirect/practical-considerations-and-recommendations-for-religious-leaders-and-faith-based-communities-in-the-context-of-covid-19

Zaami, S., Marinelli, E., & Varì, M. R. (2020). New trends of substance abuse during COVID-19 pandemic: An international perspective. *Frontiers in Psychiatry, 11.* https://doi.org/10.3389/fpsyt.2020.00700

Manufactured by Amazon.ca
Bolton, ON